A Kurdish-English Dictionary
Dialect of Sulaimania, Iraq

By
Ernest N. McCarus

Ann Arbor
The University of Michigan Press

*This work was developed pursuant to a contract between the United States
Office of Education and The University of Michigan and is published with
permission of the United States Office of Education.*

PREFACE

In 1960, the Office of Education (Department of Health, Education, and Welfare) proposed that Ernest N. McCarus, Associate Professor of the Department of Near Eastern Languages and Literatures at the University of Michigan and a recognized authority in Kurdish, begin the preparation of a Basic Course and a series of graded Readers for the instruction of students in that language. In the subsequent contracts between the Office of Education and the University, Professor McCarus was designated "Principal Investigator."

With the hearty cooperation of the Ministry of Education of the Republic of Iraq, Professor McCarus obtained for two years (1960-1962) the services of a native Kurdish scholar, originally of Sulaimania, Iraq, Mr. Jamal J. Abdulla, then teaching (and currently Lecturer) in the Higher Institute of Languages of the University of Baghdad. Mr. Abdulla became Co-editor of the majority of the volumes produced under the contracts, selected most of the articles chosen for analysis, and under the supervision of Professor McCarus prepared for them the accompanying exercises and drills. The Department and the University hereby expresses its sincere gratitude to the Iraqi Ministry of Education and the University of Baghdad for making possible this advantageous collaboration.

The Department and the Editors give special recognition to Mrs. Jannat Sirous Balandgray, a Persian and herself a student of Kurdish, who provided significant assistance in the editorial preparations and the overall format. A similar debt must be acknowledged to three others who participated in the preparation of the manuscript: Miss Nancy Kubany, who typed the English and the Kurdish transcriptions; to Miss Selma Khammash, who typed the Kurdish text; and to Mr. Hamdi Qafisheh, who, though not possessing knowledge of Kurdish himself, painstakingly and intelligently proofread the materials.

The Department of Near Eastern Languages and Literatures is proud that one of the permanent members of its instructional and research staff, Professor McCarus, has thus brought to successful completion a series of volumes devoted to the study

of a language, Kurdish, which (though spoken by a substantial
number of people in the Near East) has received comparatively
little attention hitherto in the United States.

Ann Arbor, Michigan

May 31, 1966

George G. Cameron,

Chairman, Dept. of Near
Eastern Languages and Literatures

UNIVERSITY OF MICHIGAN PUBLICATIONS IN KURDISH

1. Jamal Jalal Abdulla and Ernest N. McCarus, Kurdish Basic Course. (Dialect of Sulaimania, Iraq), University of Michigan Press, 1967.

2. Jamal Jalal Abdulla and Ernest N. McCarus, Kurdish Readers. Volume I, Newspaper Kurdish. University of Michigan Press, 1967.

3. Jamal Jalal Abdulla and Ernest N. McCarus, Kurdish Readers. Volume II, Kurdish Essays, University of Michigan Press, 1967.

4. Jamal Jalal Abdulla and Ernest N. McCarus, Kurdish Readers, Volume III, Kurdish Short Stories, University of Michigan Press, 1967.

5. Ernest N. McCarus, A Kurdish-English Dictionary (Dialect of Sulaimania, Iraq), University of Michigan Press, 1967.

INTRODUCTION

The Basic Course follows the audio-lingual approach in teaching the phonology, basic structure, and useful vocabulary of the speech of the educated native of Sulaimania, Iraq. The writing system and an introduction to written Kurdish are included; there are tapes to accompany the lessons. The Readers assume mastery of the contents of the Basic Course and provide readings in three genres. Newspaper Kurdish contains news items and articles, with exercises for classroom drill; the other two Readers contain texts with annotations. All of the vocabulary of these four volumes is contained in this Dictionary. Included also are items from other selections from the Kurdish press, principally the newspaper Zhin, as well as expressions recorded from the speech of natives of Sulaimania, both on the spot and in this country. Thus, the language of this Dictionary is strictly that of Sulaimania, Iraq, predominantly literary, but including spoken language as well. As such, it is a reflection of Kurdish as it actually occurs in present-day Iraq.

* * * *

Kurdish in Iraq is written in a modified Arabic script. As explained in the Basic Course (pages 421-425), Kurdish script, if written in its ideal form, is nearly completely unambiguous; i.e., it is a nearly phonemic script. However, this ideal is rarely attained: conventions vary from person to person and from time to time, or are simply ignored or neglected; the result is that a given word may occur in the literature in any of several orthographic variants. For the sake of consistency and ease of reference the items in this Dictionary are arranged according to their phonemic (Romanized) transcription; alphabetic order is given on page viii. Note that in this transcription no word begins with a vowel; all vowel-initial words are listed under glottal stop (?). At the same time, the word is given in the left column in Kurdish script spelled as it was encountered in the original.

The Kurdish script and the phonemic transcription do not necessarily agree. The former represents the way a Kurd might refer to the item in question; it is generally a linguistically viable form. The transcription, on the other hand, is arranged to provide grammatical information, such as the relative order of the constituent elements of a verbal phrase, or how the direct object is expressed. Thus, the Kurdish entry might be an infinitive, while the transcription presents the same information as a phrase. دان بە...نان 'to acknowledge, recognize (a country)' is the citation form while the transcription dan bə...nán shows that the prepositional phrase containing the object (indicated by...) precedes the verb, e.g. dan bə ʔerán ʔəkən 'they recognize Iran'.

The order of presentation within each entry is as follows: the meaning of the word alone is given first; then it is given in phrases and other expressions. Translations which are largely synonymous are separated by commas; semicolons separate groups of synonyms. Verbs are listed in their infinitive form, with the present stem given in parenthesis, e.g. čun (č-) 'to go'.

Verbal phrases are listed according to the following priorities: Verbal phrases containing a noun, e.g. bas k̈ird̈in 'to discuss', are listed under that noun. If there is no noun but there is an adjective, e.g. pan k̈ird̈in 'to widen', it is entered under the adjective. Otherwise, it is listed under the verb itself, e.g. řa k̈ird̈in 'to run away', ləbər k̈ird̈in 'to put on, don'. The verbal phrases are arranged alphabetically first according to the preverbal and then the postverbals and other forms which follow the verb. The following very common verbs have been abbreviated thus:

b.	bun	b.əwə	bunəwé
d.	dan	d.əwə	danəwé
g.	g̈irẗin	g.əwə	g̈irtnəwé
k.	k̈ird̈in	k.əwə	k̈ird̈nəwé

Special attention has been given to the indication of the object of verbal clauses. The normal patterns are as follows: the object of the verbal clause whose preverbal is a noun is linked by izafa to that noun, as bas-i řega náka 'it doesn't discuss the roads'. If the preverbal is an adjective or adverb the object is indicated by its position before the preverbal, as šəqàm pán ʔəkən 'they are widening the streets' and pyaw dér ʔəka 'he removes the man'.

The object follows a preverbal preposition, as sər lə
kwe ʔədəyn? 'Where are we going to visit?' Exceptions
to these rules are indicated by the convention of suffixing
-y, representing the third singular pronominal suffix 'he',
to a noun which is translated as the subject in English,
as lə ---y b. 'to remember', where --- stands for bir
'memory'. Thus, lə bírtə? is translated 'Do you remember?'
(literally, "is it in your recollection?'). The object may
be expressed by -i..., wherein the object (...) is linked
by izafa (-i) to the preverbal, e.g. nĭkul-i...k. 'to
deny s.th.'; or by using three dots... to indicate the
position of the object which is given in the English as
"s.th." or "s.o.", e.g. ...ləbər k. 'to put on, don,
wear' (s.th.), where the object precedes rather than follows
the preposition.

Other conventions are
--- indicates repetition of the basic entry.
( ) indicates optional omission.

Since the sequences wĭ-and wʊ-, are both pronounced wʊ-
the latter transcription is used in this book since it
also coincides with Kurdish script.

The combination -yə- is pronounced -ye-; both spellings
ﻪ and ﻲ occur in Kurdish script, and both transcriptions
are used here.

Initial consonant clusters, as pr-, sn-, fr-, etc. are
for the most part arbitrarily spelled with -i-, as pír-,
sin-, fir-, etc.

Abbreviations:

agric.	agriculture	k.	kirdín 'to make'
b.	bun 'to be'	m.p.n.	masc. pers. name
conj.	conjunction	mil.	military
d.	dan 'to give'	n.	noun
dial.	dialectal	onom.	onomatopoeia
dim.	diminutive	part.	participle
exclam.	exclamation	pass.	passive voice
f.p.n.	feminine personal name	pres.	present tense
fig.	figurative	pron.	pronominal
foll.	following	prov.	proverb
g.	girtín 'to take'	subj.	subject
imperat.	imperative	subjunct.	subjunctive
inf.	infinitive	suff.	suffix
interj.	interjection	Sul.	Sualimania
intr.	intransitive	var.	variant
		voc.	vocative

The alphabetic order observed here is as follows:

ʔ ʕ a b č d e ə f g

ɣ h h̲ i ï ɪ j k l l̲

m n ŋ o p q r ř s š

s̲ t u ʊ v w x y z ž

ئــا   ʔá   yes; ah, yes! indeed!

ئابرور   ʔabrú   shame, modesty; honor --- bïrdín to dishonor, disgrace

ئابو هـه وا   ʔabuhəwá   climate

ئابوری   ʔaburí   economy, economics; economic

ئاد ه می زاد   ʔàdəmizád   human being, mankind, man

ئافیریم   ʔáferim, ʔáferin   bravo!

ئافرهت   ʔafrét   woman

ئاگــا   ʔagá   attention, care, heed. ---t lə číyə. what do you know! --- lə...bún to be aware of. ---y lə gïftugóbu He was aware of the conversation.

ئاگادار   ʔagadár lə   aware of, careful about. lə...əwə --- k. to be careful about

آگاداری   agadarí   awareness, care, attention. ləmbabətəwə agadarí- zyad   more awareness on this matter

ئاگاده ری   ʔagadərí   information

ئاگــر   ʔagír   fire.--- d. to set fire

ئاگردان   ʔagïrdán   fireplace

ئاغــا   ʔaɣá   Agha (title given to feudal lords and to big land owners)

ئاهـه نگ   ʔahéŋ   entertainment, party; festival

ئاجیل و ماجیل   ʔajilumajíl   devils, demons

ئالــیك   ʔalík   forage

ئالــــرور   ʔalú   tonsils

ئــال   ʔál   pink; dark red

ئــالا   ʔalá   flag, banner

1

ئالات	ʔalát tools, implements
ئالو کوڕ	ʔalugóř exchange; change
ئاڵ ووالَا	ʔáluwala multicolored, colorful
ئامـاده	ʔamadé ready. --- k. to make ready, prepare
ئامانـج	ʔamánj target, goal; purpose, object, aim, intent
ئامـوزا	amozá cousin
ئانیشـك	ʔaníšk elbow
ئارا	ʔarám patience. --- g. to be patient, be still. --- lə...bïrrán, ---y ləbər bïrrán (pass. of bïrín) to lose all patience
ئاراسته	ʔarasté direction. --- k. to direct s.o. to
ئاراسته که ر	ʔarastəkér steering, guiding
ئارد	ʔárd flour
ئاره زوو	ʔarəzu choice, desire. ---i xótə as you wish. bə--- by desire, on purpose. --- k. to wish, desire to
ئاره زوو که ر	ʔarəzukér desirous, wishful
ئـاره ق	ʔaréq sweat. --- k.əwə to sweat
ئـارو	ʔarú cucumber
ئـاس	as ace (cards)
ئاسـا	ʔasá like
ئاسـایی	ʔasaí imitation. xotạn --- just like you, just as you (did it). řadə-i---- average amount
ئاسـان	ʔasán simple; easy. --- k. to simplify
ئاسـانی	ʔasaní facility, ease. bə --- easily
ئاسایش	ʔasayíš peace; safety, security
آسك	ʔasík deer, gazelle

ئاسن   ʔasín   iron (metal)

ئاسنگەڕی   ʔasíngərí   blacksmithery

آســـیا   ʔasıyá   Asia

آسمان   ʔasmán   sky. ---i dur lə zəwíəwə   outer space

آسمانــــی   ʔasmaní   of the sky, heavenly; blue, azure; space (adj.)

ئاســـــو   ʔasó¹   horizon

ئاســـــو   ʔasó²   Aso (m.p.n.)

ئاســـتەم   ʔastém   harm

ئاســودە   ʔasudé   tranquil; comfortable. --- k. to make comfortable

ئاسودەیی   ʔasudəí   happiness; prosperity. kəwtnə ---əwə They became prosperous. bə --- leisurely, comfortably

ئاســـیا   ʔasyá = ʔasıyá   Asia

ئاش   ʔaš   mill

ئاشەوان   ʔašəwán   miller

اشکـــرا   ʔaškǐrá   clear, obvious. bə --- clearly, openly, overtly

ئاشنـــا   ʔašná   expertness

ئاشـــت   ʔašt   peaceful, friendly. --- b.əwə to be reconciled

آشتی   ʔaští   peace. --- dway šəř xóšə. Peace after fighting is pleasant. (prov.)

ئاشـوری   ʔašurí   Assyrian

ئاـــاو   ʔáw   water. --- dán bə to water, irrigate. --- zanə dém (ze-) water flows to the mouth; to drool

آوا   ʔawa¹   sunset. --- b. to set (sun); to disappear (fig.)

3

ئـاوا	ʔawáˀ inhabited. --- k.əwə to make habitable; to develop, construct
ئـاوادان	ʔawadán = ʔawədán prosperous, well-developed
ئاوایی	ʔawaí inhabited place: village, camp (civil), etc.
ئاواكردنـەوه	ʔawakïrdnəwé development, construction
ئـاواره	ʔawaré wanderer, vagabond
ئاوات	ʔawát bo aspiration, desire for. ---i díl heart's desire. --- xwastin bo to aspire to, desire for
ئـاواتـەخـواز	awatəxwáz hopeful
ئـاواز	ʔawáz tune, melody
ئاودان	ʔawdán irrigation
ئـاوینـه	ʔawené mirror
ئـاوەدان	ʔawədán = ʔawadán prosperous, well-developed
آوەدانـی	ʔawədaní inhabitedness; civilization, prosperity (of a country)
آوەل	ʔawél friend; companion
ئاوی شـەكـراو	ʔawišəkráw syrup
ئاور دانـەوه	ʔawïr lə... danəwé to glance around at
ئاوریشم	ʔawríšïm silk
ئاورشین	ʔawrïšén sprinkling, spray (with water)
ئـاوس	ʔaws pregnant
ئاوسان	ʔawsán (ʔawse-) to swell; to warp (intr.)
	ʔáy 0! hey!

4

ئــاخ   ʔáx   oh!   alas!

ئاخــــر   ʔaxír   well now!   after all!   come now!
--- nábe   come now--that won't do!

ئاخـــری   ʔaxïrí   last, final

ئاخر و ئوخر   ʔaxïruʔoxír   at the end of (year,etc.)

ئــای   ʔay   ah!

ئایــا   ʔáya (interrog., literary Kurdish; not translated in direct questions). In indirect questions: whether. kə--- as to whether...

آیــەت   ʔayét (pl.: ʔayát) a verse in the Koran

آیین   ʔayín   religion

ئاینده   ʔayïndé   coming, next, following (of time)

ئاینی   ʔayïní   religious

آزا   ʔazá   brave.   --- k.   to encourage

ئازا   ʔaza   Aza (m.p.n.)

ئازادی   ʔazadí   freedom

ئازایـی   ʔazaí   bravery, courage

ئازار   ʔazár   severe pain

ئازایانه   ʔazáyane   courageously, bravely

ئـێ   ʔé   o.k.,   all right; yes, go on! (I'm lis-
tening)

ئیجگار   ʔejgár   completely; very much

ایــل   ʔel   nation, people

ئیمــا   ʔemé   (indep. pron.)   we; us

ئیــران   ʔeran   Iran

ئیرانـــی   ʔeraní   Iranian

ئــــیره   ʔeré   here (as subject).   --- xoše.   It's nice
here.   kéy hati bo ---   when did you come
here? leré   in this place, here. leréwe
from here, hence.

5

ئیسك	ʔesk, (= ʔesqan) bone(s).---súk beautiful. ---qúrs ugly
ئیستـان	ʔesqán bone
ئیستـا	ʔestá now; at present. suryá-i ʔesta present-day Syria. ---š even now. lə --- wə from now, as of now
ئیستگـه	ʔestgé station (broadcasting, railway). ---i řadyói bəritanyá B.B.C.
ئیستـر	ʔestír mule
ئیش	ʔeš pain
ئیـواره	ʔewaré, ʔewaré evening. ---t baš good evening! šéš-i --- six p.m.
ئیوه	ʔewé you (pl)
ئیستكه	ʔezgé = ʔestgé station
ئهعمار	ʔeʕmár public works. məjlıs-i --- The Development Board
ئهبسی	ʔəbé must: see bún
ئهبـو	ʔəbú it was necessary that...: see bún
ئهدهب	ʔədéb literature
ئهدهبسی	ʔədəbí literary
ئهدیب	ʔədíb literary figure, writer, man of letters
ئهفهندی	ʔəfəndí any person who wears western clothes; gentleman
ئهفریقیا ، ئه فریقا	ʔəfriqyá, ʔəfriqá Africa
ئهفسـوس	ʔéfsos alas!
ئهگهر	ʔəgér if (foll. by pret. = more likely; foll. by subjunct. = less likely) --- hát if he comes. --- bet if he should come. --- bétu if, in the event that... ---hatu if, in the event that... --- nébwayə had it not been for...
ئهگهرچی	ʔəgərčí even though, even if

ئەگینـا   ʔəginá (foll. by imperf. for contrary to fact result) otherwise. --- némzani otherwise I wouldn't have known it.

اهالـــى   ʔəhalí people, civilian population (pl)

ئەهـــل   ʔəhïl inhabitants, residents

ئەهریمەن   ʔəhrimén Ahriman, the Zoroastrian spirit of darkness and evil

ئەحـــە   ʔəhé dim. of ʔəhméd 'Ahmad'

ئەحمەد، احمد   ʔəhméd Ahmad (m.p.n.)

أحـــرار   ʔəhřár liberals

ئەلەمانـــى   ʔələmaní German

ئەلەپەشە   ʔələ pəšé Aalapasha (m.p.n.)

ئەم   ʔəm this (pron.); this one. bèlam --- lə hïzb-i dimuqratíyə but this one is from the Democratic Party. peš --- after this, subsequently. pl.: ʔéman these (cf. ʔəmé, ʔəw)

ئەمـــان   ʔéman (pl. of ʔəm) these (pron.)

ئەمانە   ʔəmané these (pron.; more specific than ʔéman)

ئەمارەت   ʔəmarét emirate, principality. ʔəmarètədə-rəbəgəkán the feudal principalities

ئەمە   ʔəmé this (pron.), this one, this thing. bo --- for this, therefore. ləməwpéš before now, ago

ئەم ... ە   ʔém...ə̀, ʔém...yə̀ this (adj)

ئەمەتا   ʔəmətá here it is. --́ yanə̀ here is the club

امریکـــا   ʔəməriká America

ئەمەریکـــى، امریکى   ʔəmərikí American

ئەمین   ʔəmin Amin (m.p.n.)

ئەمجـــا   ʔémja then, after that

7

ئه‌مرو   ʔə́mřo = ʔímro   today

ئه‌موستیله‌   ʔəmustilé   ring, finger ring

ئه‌ندام   ʔəndám   member

ئه‌ندامی   ʔəndamí   membership (in an organization). mawè-i --- term of membership, term of office

ئه‌ندازیار   ʔəndazyár   engineer

ئه‌ندۆنیسیا   ʔə̀ndonisyá   Indonesia

ئه‌نجام   ʔənjám   result (of: bo). be --- ineffective, inconsequential. lə ---́ da in the end, finally. lə ---i...b. to be a result of, result from...

ئه‌نجومه‌ن   ʔənjumén   council, board, committee

ئه‌قل   ʔə́qïḻ   mind; intelligence, reason. --- wéryan ʔəgrè the mind will accept them, i.e., they are reasonable

ئه‌ری   ʔəré   yes; well, now! (may indicate change of subject)

ئه‌رک   ʔə́rk   arduous work; toil, hardship

ئه‌رمه‌نی   ʔərməní   Armenian

ئه‌وا   ʔəwá   there, in that place; there was...; then, in that case

ئه‌رز   ʔə́rz   earth; land

ئه‌رزروملی   ʔərzrumlí   Arzrumli (m.p.n.)

ئه‌سپ   ʔə̆sïp, ʔə̆sp   horse

ئه‌سمه‌ر   ʔəsmə́r   brunette

السلام‌علیکم   ʔəssəlámu ʕəléykum   greetings!

ئه‌ستیره‌   ʔəsteré   star

ئه‌ستەمۆڵ   ʔəstəmíḻ   Istanbul

ئه‌ستور   ʔəstúr   thick

ewé

ئەستو ?əstó the thickest part of the neck. gírtnə
--- to assume the burden of, take charge of

أشــراف ?əšráf (Ar.) dignitaries, nobility, eminent
persons

ئەتوم ?ətóm atom. hèz-i ---́ atomic power

ئەتومى ?ətomí atomic

ئەو ?əw he; she; it(pron.). ?əw that (dem.).
---i tír the other one too. pl.: ?əwan they.
(cf. ?əwé, ?əwané, ?əm)

ئەورا ?əwá then; in that case; thereupon

ئەوان ?əwan (pl. of ?əw) they

ئەوانه ?əwané (pl. of ?əwə) those (pron.) ---i
(foll. by subjunct.) those who

ئەوى ?əwé that place (as subj.), there. bó ?əwe
to that place, there, thither. ləwé in that
place, there. ləwéwə from there

ئەوه ?əwé that (dem.). lə paš ---́ after that,
then. lə paš --- kə after, after having.
hatnə sèr --- (foll. by subjunct.) to come
to the point that... Used redundantly with
kə when the latter introduces a clause which
would otherwise be the object of a preposition
or come after izafa: that (conj.). həz bəwə
?əkəm kə bínasïm I would like to meet him.
Used as expletive: hey! I say! --- lə kwé
buy! hey--where have you been? --- ?əley čí
what are you talking about! ---i (foll. by
indic.) every one who. ---i dəsti čək-i
?əgïrt every one who could bear arms. (Foll.
by subjunct.) anyone who, he who, those who,
whoever. ---i...həmúy every single one who...
---i bïčetə šar-i kwerán ?əbé désti bə čáwəwə
bïgret when in Rome do as the Romans do.
(prov.) be (bəbe) ---i (foll. by subjunct.)
without. bo ---i (foll. by subjunct.) in
order that. ləbér ---i kə in view of the
fact that, because. peš ---i (foll. by subjunct.) before (conj.) ---i kə... ?əwéyə
what is...is that...

9

ئە و ، ـە	ʔéw...ə̀ that (adj.) ---wext--- at that time. ---i (kə) the...that... léw wulatanè-i xwa in those countries where God... ʔə̀wdəmè-i kə tó láman buyt when you were (still) with us
ئە وه نـده	ʔəwəndé that much; so much; so. ---yaríman kïrdïbu zor hilakbuyn we had played so much that we got very tired. qïsəkéš her ---́ bu kə wùti all she said was... ---ʔəzanïm before I knew it... ʔəwəndéy nébïrd it was not long before... ---bəhézə it is so strong that... ---i tïr that much more, all the more
ئە وه تا	ʔəwətá there he is, there is...
او قــاف	ʔəwqáf estates in mortmain, wakfs
ئە و روپـا	ʔəwrupá Europe
ئە ور پایـسى	ʔəwropaí European
ئە و سـا	ʔə́wsa then, at that time; then, after that, afterwards. of that time, the then...
ئە وتــو	ʔə́wto such a; so much hèzek-i dïrustkèr-i ʔə́wtoyə kə is such a creative force that. kèlkek-i ʔə́wtoy nəbu it did not have much effect (foll. by subjunct.) such a...as to, of such a nature that...
ئە ووه ل ، اول	ʔəwwəl first. ---sal the first year
ئە ى	ʔéy (voc. part.) o! well, now (making a change in course of conversation). ---čón nèhatite dərəwə well then, how is it that you did not come out? ---ʔədiban-i kurdustán o men of letters of Kurdistan!
ئە یلول ، ايلول	ʔəylúl September
ئە یــوب	ʔəyúb Ayoub (m.p.n.)
ئازه ربايجـان	ʔəzïrbayján Azerbaijan
اداره	ʔidaré administration
ئيمـان	ʔimán faith

ئیستكـان   ʔistkán   glass (of)

ئیش   ʔíš   work; job; something to do. ʔémʔi-šanè   these activities --- k. to work (at a job)

ئیش كردن   ʔiškɪrdɪ́n   working, work

ایشوكار   ʔišukár   function(s), duty, duties; work, job

ئیتـر   ʔitɪ́r   then, at that point; what is more, moreover

ئیبقا بون لـه   ʔɪbqa bún lə   to fail in (a subject, course)

ابراهیم   ʔɪbrahím   Abraham

ابتدائـى   ʔɪbtidaʔí   primary, elementary

افتاده   ʔɪftadé   crippled; diseased

اهتمام   ʔɪhtimam bə... dán   to attach importance to; concern

احصــاء   ʔɪhṣá   statistics

ئه مجا   ʔímja   then, afterwards

امـلا   ʔɪmlá   dictation

ئیمپریالـیزم   ʔɪmpɪ̌ryalízm   imperialism

ئیمـرو   ʔímřo   today

ئیمروژ   ʔímřož = ʔímřo   today

ئیمتحان   ʔɪmtiḥán   examination. --- sər-i ṣá̱l

final exam

ئینجا   ʔínja   then, --- ... ya (foll. by subjunct.) whether...or

انسـان   ʔɪnsán   person, human being

ئینگلــترا   ʔïŋgɪ̌ltəra   England

اقتـراح   ʔɪqtɪ̌ráẖ   suggestion, proposal

ئیسـلام   ʔɪslám   ɪslam

ليسراحەت	ʔɪsrahḗt rest, break. --- k. to rest, take a rest
استعمار	ʔɪstï°mắr imperialism; imperialists (coll.)
استعمارچى	ʔɪstï°marčí imperialist
استعمارى	ʔɪstï°marí imperialist
ئيتـــر	ʔɪtír = ʔitír then
انگلــــيزى	ʔŋlizí, ʔïnglizí English; English language
ئوغـر	ʔoɣúr be (pl.: bïn) where are you going? (honorific). --- k. to travel (honorific)
ئوردو	ʔordú army
ئوستا	ʔostá master, craftsman
ئوتوموبيل	ʔotomobíḷ; ʔutumbíḷ car; auto
ئوتّؤمّؤبيلچى	ʔotomobilčí chauffeur; driver, motorist
ئوميد	ʔumḗd hope. --- k. to hope, hope for. ---y həyə (foll. by subjunct.) to have hopes (to do s.th.). ʔumḗdtan həyə xïzmḗt-i wuḷatəkḗtan bkən you hope to serve your country. naʔumḗd hopeless(ness)
أوتيل	ʔutḗl hotel
اصولـــى	ʔuṣulí formal; as a formality, routine
ئوتوميبل	ʔutumbíḷ automobile

ع

عــادەت	°adḗt custom, habit; tradition
عــادل	°adíl Adil (m.p.n.)
عالــم	°alḗm world; people. ʔḗm ---ə həmúy all of these people
عەجزى	°ajzí sadness

12

عاقڵ	ᶜaqíḻ reasonable; sensible
طارفى ئالّى	ᶜarf-i ʔaḻé ᶜArif ᶜAle (m.p.n.)
عاسمان	ᶜasmán = ʔasmán sky. ču bə ---a he jumped up in the air
عاست	ᶜást (specific) position, place. le ---i xóm in my position, right where I was
عاستم	ᶜastə́m: bə--- hardly, barely
عاشـق	ᶜašíq lover. ᶜašíq-i ... b. to fall in love with; to be enchanted by
عەبا	ᶜəbá aba, cloak-like woolen wrap (usually worn by women)
عەباسـى	ᶜəbasí Abbasid
عبد الكـريم	ᶜəbdulkərim Abdul-Karim (m.p.n.)
عبد المجـيد	ᶜə̀bdulməjíd Abdul-Majid (m.p.n.)
عبد القـادر	ᶜə̀bdulqadír Abdul-Qadir (m.p.n.)
عبد الرحمان	ᶜə̀bdurrəhmán Abdul-Rahman (m.p.n.)
عليكم السـلام	ᶜəléykumussəlám (Ar.) greetings (in response to ʔəssəlàmuᶜəléykum)
عطـى	ᶜəlí Ali (m.p.n.)
عەلى شيش	ᶜəli- šíš turkey
عەمادىيه	ᶜəmadıyé Amadia (city in northern Iraq)
عەنتيكـه	ᶜəntiké antique
عەنتيكەخانه	ᶜəntikəxané museum
عەرەب	ᶜəréb Arab
عەرەبـى	ᶜərəbí Arabic; Arabic language
عەرز	ᶜərz = ʔərz land, soil; earth
عەســر	ᶜésïr afternoon

13

عسكـر   ʕəskér soldier

عسكرى   ʕəskərí military, army (adj.)

عـيب   ʕəyb shame, disgrace. --- k. to be ashamed. --- nákəy? have you no shame?

عـين   ʕəyn-i the same. ʕəyn-i təléb the same request

عـزيز   ʕəzíz Aziz (m.p.n.)

عـيراقى   ʕiraqí Iraqi

عيسى   ʕisá Jesus

عـلمى   ʕïlmí scientific

عـود   ʕud lute

عـورف   ʕúrf convention, common custom

عـمر   ʕumér Omar (m.p.n.)

عوسمانى   ʕusmaní Ottoman

b

بـا   bá1 air, wind

بـا   bá2(cohortative part. foll. by subjunct.) let's, let... --- xerá bŕoyn let's go quickly. --- hər qsə nékəm I'd better not say anything

بابان   babán Baban, a Kurdish ruling family in the days of the Ottoman Empire

بابـه   bábə (voc.) daddy!

بابـت   babét kind, sort. lə ---...(əwə) about, concerning

بـا د ه   badé wine

بادينانى   badinaní of Badinan, Badinani

بـاغ   baγ, bax garden

14

باهـــــو   bahú   the arms and shoulders (character- istic of strength)

بایی   baí   the worth of, for (the price of). --- pənjá pul   50 fils worth of...

بــلّا   balá   height.   --- həlčú tall

بالابـرز   balabérz   tall (an attribute of feminine beaūty)

بالـــندﮦ   balĭndé   bird

بـــام   bám (cohortative part., foll. by subjunct.) = bá   let's

بامـیه   bamyé   okra

بـــان   ban¹   roof.   --- əkəw dú həwa   one roof and two (opposite) breezes (prov. in ref. to partiality or discrimination)

بـــان   ban²   plateau.   bàn-i ʔerán   the Iranian Plateau

بانـــد   bánd   band (music).   ---i mosiqà-i ʕəskərí   military band

بانگ   baŋ   call; invitation; call to prayer.   --- k.   to call s.o.; to invite s.o.

بابـــیر   bapír   grandfather

باتـــی   baqí   change (money)

بــــار   bár¹   situation, condition, state.   ---i ʔaburí   the economic situation. bém barè-i ʔestáy   in its present state

بــــار   bár²   burden; load

بـــاران   barán¹   rain.   --- ʔəbaret   it rains. tĭrs-i barán man nébu   we weren't afraid it would rain

بــــاران   barán²   Baran (m.p.n.)

بـــاران بارین   baranbarín   rainfall

بـــارﮦ   baré: lə ---i...əwe   on the subject of, concerning

بـارهكا   barəgá   royal palace

بـاريـك   barík   thin; slender

بـاريـن   barín (bar-)   to rain.   barán ʔəbaret it rains

بـاس   bás   discussion; information, conversation; subject, topic.   --- k.   to talk about, discuss.   ---i čí ʔəka   What is he talking about?

بـاسـه   basé   subject

بـاسكتبـول   baskïtból   basketball

بـاش   baš   good; well (adv.).   bə --- zanín (foll. by subjunct.)   to deem it worthwhile (to do s.th.); to (do s.th.) by choice

باشـى   baš5   goodness.   bə --- well, thoroughly. ʔəbé kurdí bə --- fer bi   you must learn Kurdish thoroughly

بـات : ده بـاتـى   bat: lə báti   instead of

بـاوهرر   bawéř   belief, conviction.   --- k.   to believe.   --- b. bə   to trust, have confidence in

بـاوهش   bawéš   bosom; armful.   --- gïrtín   to embrace

بـاوك   bawk   father

بـاخ   báx   garden; orchard

بـازار   bazár   market, bazaar

بـازرگان   bazïrgán   dry goods merchant, draper

بـى   be, bəbé, be...əwə   without (often used with nouns to form adjectival or adverbial expressions, as: be quwét weak; --- sud   useless; in vain; (these expressions can then receive the suffix -í to form a noun, as: beʔiší unemployment; bə ho-i befərhəŋíəwə   for the lack of a dictionary)

16

بى ئيشى   be?iší   unemployment

بى بەش كردن   bebəš kïrdín lə   to deprive s.o. of

بى دەنگى   bedəŋí   silence

بيگانە   begané   foreign; alien

بى كارى   bekarí   unemployment

بيروح   beróh   inanimate (object)

بێشە ، بێشكە   bešé, beškḗ   den, lair

بيشەلان   bešəlán   (dense) forest

بيوەژنى   bewəžïní   widowhood. bə --- in widow-hood, as a widow

بىوىسعەتى   bewɪsʕətí   lack of space, confinement

بـــيز   bez: --- hatín (foll. by subjunct.) to demean o.s. to, condescend to

بيـزار   bezar   displeased

بيـزارى   bezarí   dissatisfaction, displeasure

بـــ   bə¹ , bə...əwə   by, with, in, for. Instr.: bə́mqələmə̀wə bnusə write with this pen. in (a language): bə kurdí in Kurdish. Often used with nouns to form adjectival or adverbial expressions, as bə quwét strong; bə sardíəwə coldly

بـــ   bə²   by, beside

بـــ   bə³   (in oaths) by. -- xwá by God! really! bə sə̀r-i tó (I swear) by your head!

بەبى   bəbé = be   without

بەبە   bəbé   Bebe (epithet of the Baban princes)

بەد   béd   bad; evil

بەدم   bədə́m...əwə   along with, while (in the process of)

بـﮒ   bəg bey (inherited or honorific title of courtesy for men of high rank; follows name). ʔəmín zəki --- Amin Zaki Bey; mĭstfə bə́g-i.báwki his father Mustafa Bey

بـﮒزاده   bəgzadé son(s) or daughter(s) of a bey; an influential man

بـﻐا ، بـﻐدا   bəɣá; bəɣdá Baghdad

بـها   bəhá cost, price

بـهـار   bəhár spring (the season)

بـهـهلـدداوان   bəhəlḙdawán quickly, hurriedly, arunning

بـﻜﮭلـۆرى   bəkəlorí baccalaureate

بـﻜراوا   bəkrawá Bakrawa (p.n.)

بـﻜرهﺟـر   bəkrəjó Bakrajo (p.n.)

بـﻜرهسـور   bəkrəsúr Bakrasur (m.p.n.)

بـﻟـﻚ   bəlḙḱ licorice

بلجيـﻜا   bəljika Belgium

بـﻟـسـﻪ   bəlsé wandering, stray. --- b. to stray

بـﻼ   bəḻá calamity

بـﻼم   bέḻam but

بـﻟـﻰ   bέḻe yes

بـﻟـﻴن   bəlέn promise. --- d. bə to make a prōmise to

بـﻟـﻚ   bəḻέk spotted; leper

بـﻟﮔﻪ   bəḻgé proof; evidence

بـﻟﮔﻪ   bέḻkə = bəḻku perhaps

بـﻟﮔـو   bέḻku (foll. by subjunct.) perhaps, maybe. Contradicting previous neg.: but, on the contrary

18

بە ن   bən   string; fine cord

بە ند   bənd; bəŋ   that with which something is tied; joined firmly; bound together; article; chapter. --- b. to remain, stay. --- k. to bind, tie down

بە ندە   bəndə́   servile; slave

بە ندەگی   bəndəgí   slavery, servitude

بە ندەخوین   bəndəxwén   cord used as belt for trousers

بە ندی   bəndí   prisoner

بە ندیخانە   bəndixané   prison

بنزینخانە   bənzinxané   gasoline station

بە نگ بە   bəŋé bə   dependent on

بە پیتی   bəpití   fertility

بە قەد   bəqə́d   in proportion to, commensurate with

بە ر   bər[1]   on: see ləbér   because of. --- b.əwə sər.., to drop, fall down on. ---i...kəwtin to fall on, hit, strike s.th.

بە ر   bér[2] before. lə ---(da) in front of, before. --- lə before (time). --- ləwə-i (foll. by subjunct.) before (conj.). lémow--- heretofor, previous-ly, before today. bərtír former

بە ر   bér[3] beside, by. --- b. to flee, escape

بە ر   bər[4]: bər-i...g. to cover. shroud s.th. ---i ʔasmáni girt it covered up the skies. kəwtnə -´- to take in, be covered by s.th. (e.g., land is flooded over by water)

بە ر   bər[5], bérekə yield, produce (agric.). --- g. to bear fruit

به رامهر	bərambér toward; opposite. --- bə before, in front of; against. --- k. to compare, match up s.th.
به ران	bərán ram
به راز	bəráz pig
به ربانگ	bərbáŋ meal, supper
به ربه ره کانـی	bərbərəkané outbraving; defiance; challenge. --- k. to confront, struggle against, defy
به ربه ست	bərbést dam, barrier
به ربون	bərbún release; setting free; freeing
به رچای	bərčaí breakfast
به رد	bérd stone
به رد ه لانی	bərdəlaní stony, rocky
به ده م	bərdém: lə ---i...da in the forefront of, at the head of (procession)
به رد ه رگا	bərdərgá space immediately before the door
به رد ه رك	bərdérk-i in front of (a large building)
به رد ه ست	bərdést attendant, servant
به رد ه وام بوون	bərdəwam bún tya to be persistent, persevere in
به رد ریژ	bərdréž pavement
به ریکه	béreka, bér (agricultural) produce, yield; fruit
به ریوه بردن	bərewə bǐrdín (bə-) to manage, administer, run (an organization)
به ریوه به ر	bərewəbér manager, director, person in charge
به ریوه به رایه تی	bərewəbərayətí administration; directorate, agency. --- gǐští directorate general

بەرێوەبردن   bərewəbïrdín   management, administration

بەرێز   bəréz   respected

بەرە   bəré   offspring, progeny. be --- fruit-less; barren

بەرەبەیان   bərəbəyán   dawn; early morning hours

بەرەجوت   bərəjút   acre

بەرەکەت   bərəkét   blessing(s). ---da fortunate-ly, as luck would have it

بەرەللا   bərəllá   loose

بەرەنگار   bərəŋár   confrontation. --- b. to con-front, clash with. --- wəstán (wəst-) to stand up to, defy. híčštek níyə bərəŋári bïwəstet   there is nothing that can stand up to it

بەرەنگاربوون   bərəŋarbún   a clash, encounter

بەرەو   bérəw   towards. --- sahé ʔəčïn they are going toward the square. --- dwá backwards. --- xwár downwards. --- žur upward, up. --- žur b.əwé to go uptown

بەرگ   bérg   dress, apparel, clothes

بەرگر   bərgïr   defense

بەرهەلست   bərhəlïst   defense

بەرهەم   bərhém   fruit, produce (agric.). --- henán (hen-) to grow, raise, rear s.th. henánə --- to render s.th. productive

بەرهەم هینەر   bərhèmhenér   fruitful, productive

بەریتانیا   bəritanyá   Britain

بەرکوش   bərkóš   apron

بەرلەوە   bérləwə-i kə (foll. by subjunct.) before (conj.)

بەرمال   bərmál   prayer rug

21

به رنامه	bərnamé program
به ريا كردن	bərpá k. to stir up, provoke (an argument, etc.)
به رقی یه	bərqıyé telegram. --- k. to send a telegram
به رتیل	bərtíl bribe. --- xwardín (xo-), --- wər g. to take a bribe
به روار	bərwár castle
به رز	bérz high; lofty; elegant; eminent; elevated; refined. bə dəŋ-i --- in a loud voice. --- b.əwé to rise, ascend; to ring out
به رزه پی هه لسان	bərzəpè həl sán (s-) to stand up erect; to stand up on one's feet. bərzəpé lə-bərïm hél sa he stood up for me (out of respect)
به رزی	bərzí elevation; refinement, culture
به راورد	bəřawírd comparison. --- k. ləgəl to compare s.th. with
به ره	bəřé rug
به ررو	bəřú (pl. bəřwán) oak; acorn
به رخ	bərx lamb
به رز	bərz high, lofty. bə čawek-i --- təmašáy kïrd he regarded him highly
به رژه وه ندی	bəržəwəndí interest
به س	bəs enough, sufficient. bésmə that's enough for me. bésə! that's enough! stop it!
به سه ر...دا	bəsér... da over; around
به سه رهات	bəsərhát adventures, experiences
به سه زمان	bəsəzmán, bəsïzmán poor, wretched
به سه زمان	bəsïzmán poor; miserable, wretched

22

به سراو	bəsráw = bəstráw tied, tied up
به ست	bést dam
به سته ك	bəsték package
به سته لاك	bəstəlák frozen
به ستن	bəstín (bəst-) to tie s.th.; to convene, hold (a meeting). pass.: bəstrán bə to be tied to; to be contingent upon. --- bə...əwə to adjoin; to tie; connect s.th. to
به ستراو به	bəstráw bə tied, linked to, contingent upon
به ستو	bəstú frozen stiff; numb
به ش	béš part; section; share, lot. hətá du ---i šéw ʔəřwa until the night is two-thirds over. lə ---i zorí for the most part. --- k. to divide, share. ---i... k. to suffice, be sufficient for...
به شدار	bəšdár partner; subscriber; partaker. --- b. lə... to take part, participate in
به شداری	bəšdarí lə participation in
به شینه وه	bəšinəwé (bəš-) to distribute
به شكم	béškïm, bésku (foll. by subjunct.) perhaps
به صراوی	bəsrawí of Basra; native of Basra
به تال بوون	bətál b. to be exhausted; to come to an end
به تالسی	bətalí idleness
به خش	bəxš donation, giving
به خشين	bəxšín (bəxš-) to forgive. bïmbéxšə excuse me! pe --- to give s.th. as a gift to s.o., to present s.th. to s.o.

23

به‌خشیش   bəxšíš   prize, reward

به‌خشنده‌گی   bəxšĭndəgí   generosity; bounty

به‌خت   béxt[1]   luck, good luck.   ---y kranəwə (pass. of k.əwé)   to be lucky, have a stroke of good luck

به‌خت کردن   bəxt[2]   --- k.   to sacrifice

به‌ختووه‌ر   bəxtəwér   lucky

به‌ختیاری   bəxtiyarí   luck, good fortune; prosperity

به‌یان   bəyán   statement; declaration

به‌یانسی   bəyaní   morning; in the morning; tomorrow morning

له‌ به‌ینی   bəyn: lə béyn-i...(da)   between; among

به‌ز   bəz   fat (n.).   ---i mrišík   fat of the chicken

به‌بی به‌زه‌یی   bəzəí: bəbé ---   mercilessly, ruthlessly

به‌زین   bəzín (bəz-): da --- (lə)   to descend (from), get off (of). həḻ ---   to hop

به‌زم   bézĭm   pleasurable activities; hilarity; gaiety; party; scene, spectacle.   ---ek-i xóš   merrymaking

به‌ز مووه‌زم   bəzmuřəzm   party, partying, funmaking

بیبه‌ر   bibér, bibĭr   pepper

بینین   binín (bin-)   to see

بیر   bir[1]   well (n.)

بیر   bir[2]   thought, idea; reflection; memory; reminiscence, recollection; mind. ?əm---é kĭžu lawézə   this idea is dull and weak. ---i máləwə   homesickness. ---i máləwə k.   to be homesick. lə ---y b.   to remember, recall. báš ---yəti   he remembers it well. ?əwsəyraném lə ---ə   I remember that picnic. --́-tə či kra?   do you recall what was done? lə

--- čunəwə to forget. lə ---ḯm ǧubowə
I had forgotten it. bə ---da hatin to
imagine, think. way bə ---a hat kə...
it occurred to him that... hər ləgəl
wušə-i babán...hat bə bḯra with the
mere mention of the word Baban...began
to run through my mind. ...y kəwtnə ---
řawəžiškəkéy kəwtə bir she thought of
the "hedgehog-hunt". ---i...k. to reflect on. ---i řunak-i dwařóž kḯrdnəwé
to reflect clearly on the future. ---
lə...k., k.əwé to think of, recall,
mention s.th. --- xḯstnəwé (xə-) to
remind s.o. of

بيــــيره | biré beer

بيره وه ری | birəwərí commemoration; remembrance

بير كرد نه وه | birkḯrdnəwé thinking, reasoning (n.),
reflection

بير و | biró eczema

بير و باوه ر | bìrubawéř belief; idea, opinion; prin-
ciple; creed; ideology

بير و را | biruřá opinion; belief, idea

بيست | bḯst twenty. -́- həzar twenty thou-
sand. -́-u čwár twenty-four. -́-u yék
twenty-one

بيستن | bistín (byə-, by-; pass. bistr-) to hear

بيتاقـــه | bitaqé ticket; card. ---i həybéxt
lottery ticket

بچوك | bḯčúk small, little

بـــــلاو | bḯláw spreading; scattered. --- b.əwé
to spread (intr.). --- k. to scatter,
spread s.th.; to publish. --- k.əwé to
spread s.th.; to make known, announce;
to publish s.th.; to broadcast, transmit
(news)

بــلا و بو نه وه | bḯlawbunəwé spread, diffusion

بــلاوه كـرد ن | bḯlawé le k. to disperse

25

bḯlawəí

بـلاوه ی لی کردن	bḯlawəí le k. to disperse, scatter (intrans.)
بـلاو کردنه وه	bḯlawkḯrdnəwə́ spreading (n.), diffusion
بلــبل	bḯlbḯl, bulbúl nightingale
بلـیمهت	bḯlimə́t genius
بلــورر	bḯlúr glass, crystal
بلـیون	bḯlyún billion
بلــند	bḯlínd high. --- b. to arise, soar. --- k. to exalt, raise, elevate
بلــندی	bḯlíndí elevation, loftiness
بن	bḯn bottom. ---...(əwə) beside, next to. lə ---...da at the bottom of, under; beside, next to, near
بنـا کردن	bḯná k. to construct, build
بناغـه	bḯnaγə́ foundation. --- d.əwə́ to lay the foundations (for construction)
بناوان	bḯnawán weir, irrigation dam
بنچینهیی	bḯnčinəí basic, fundamental
بن دار	bḯndár bottom part of a tree; space immediately under a tree
بنیسی	bḯnesí flimsiness, feebleness; flimsy
بنیشت	bḯnéšt chewing gum
بنـه	bḯnə́ building
بنه ره تی	bḯnərətí basic, radical
بنه ره ت	bḯnərə́t the very roots or foundation
بنه وشه	bḯnəwšə́ violet (flower)
بنــج	bḯnj root
بنکـه	bḯnkə́ base; stronghold

بن راو   bïnřáw   the terminal point or end of a hunt or chase. cf. sərřáw

بانـی بنوگ   bïnúg: ban-i bïnúg Bani Binug (a village in Hawraman)

بریك   bïr: bïrek lə a chunk of; some of

بـرا   bïrá brother. --- két your brother. bïrayinə (voc. pl.) o brethren!

برابـش   bïrabéš co-partners

برادەر   bïradér friend

برایەتـی   bïrayetí brotherhood

برازا   bïrazá nephew

برازاوا   bïrazawá best man (in a wedding party)

براژن   bïražín brother's wife, sister-in-law

برایم پاشا   bïrayım pašá Ibrahim Pasha

برازا   bïrazá brother's children; fraternal nephew(s) or niece(s). bïrayım pašá-i ---y his nephew Ibrahim Pasha

بردن   bïrdín (-bə-) to carry,take; to take s.o. somewhere; to confiscate. ʔəyba bo dukán he takes it to the shop. to take (time). šaŋzé səʕati bïrd lə ŋyuyórkəwə bo bəɣá it took 16 hours from New York to Baghdad. ---ə...əwə to take, carry s.th. to... ---əsér to pass, spend (time). həmú layek bə xoší řoz-i jəžnəkéy ʔəbïrdəsér everybody would spend the holiday happily

بردنەوهـ   bïrdnəwé (bə-)   lə to take away, remove; to win...from. sí filsït bïrdótəwə you've won 30 fils

بریتی   bïrét: lə ---i instead of, on behalf of, for. ---i bún lə to consist, be composed of. bïretí consisting of

لەبرەوا بوون   lə bïrəwa bún to flourish, thrive

bïrín¹ (br-) to wound

27

برين	bïrín² wound, injury
برينــدار	bïrindar k. to wound, injure
برينــدار كردن	bïrindarkïrdín wounding, injuring (n.)
برين پيچ	bïrinpéč a person who dresses wounds in the hospital; male nurse
بريقانه وه	bïriqanəwé (briqe-) to shine, glitter, glisten
بريقه	bïriqé glitter, glimmer
بريقه دار	bïriqədár shining, gleaming, glistening
برنج	bïrínj rice
برنجوك	bïrïnjók gauze
برو	bïró eyebrow
برس كردن	bïrs k.əwə to raise, lift up
برسى	bïrsí the person who is hungry; the hungry one; hunger. -́-mə I am hungry. ---t níyə aren't you hungry?
برسيەتى	bïrsıyətí hunger
برووسكه	bïruské lightning; gleam
برژان	bïržán (bïrže-) to roast (intr.), be roasted. zór bïbïržet ya kém? (do you want) it to roast a lot or a little?
برژاندن	bïržandín (bïržen-) to roast, grill s.th.
برژانگ	bïržáŋ eyelash
بركردن	bïř a short piece of wood; a cut, slice. --- k. to be able to do s.th. (usually, to walk a great distance); to reach. ta čáw bïřka as far as the eye could see
بران	bïřán to be finished, at an end. dó bïřa the do is all gone. ʔáw bïřawə there's no more water. lə... --- to break with (a friend). gélek salə ʔəynasïm, bélam ʔesta lek (= léyek) bïřawin I've known him for many years, but we're now split up

برانەوە   bïřanəwé (bře-) to finish, come to an end; to cease, stop s.th. bïřayəwə it's finished, it's all over. bíbřenəwə! finish it! = stop talking!

برربرره   bïřbïřé backbone

بررین   bïřín (bř-) to cut s.th.; to cut in two, divide; to disconnect; to cover (a distance); to travel, pass through(a stage, period, etc.). da --- to cut off; to carve out; to separate. dər --- to disclose, reveal, announce. déri bři kə ?əce bo fərənsá he revealed that he is going to go to France

بررینەوە   bïřinəwé (bř-) to cut off, cut away. bo...--- to set aside, allot (money) for... Pass.: hézi bïrranəwé one's strength gives out completely

بروا   bïřwá belief, conviction. ləsər --- b. kə to be of the belief that. mïn ləsər ?əw---yəm kə... I am of the opinion that... --- bə...k. to believe in

برریار   bïřyár decision; resolution. --- d. (foll. by subjunct.) to decide, resolve (to do s.th.). --- d. ləsər to decide upon...

بست   bïst span (measurement)

بستە   bïsté pistachio

بزن   bïzín goat

بزمار   bïzmár nail

بزنەکوی   bïznəkewí ibex

بزوتنەوە   bïzutnəwé[1] (bzu-) to move; to rise

بزوتنەوە   bïzutnəwé[2] rise, movement

بزار   bïžár weeding (n.); eradication, elimination (of harmful elements). --- k. to weed out, cleanse

هەلبژاردن   bïžardín (bžer-): həl --- to select; to elect

29

بژارکردن   bĭžarkĭrdĭn   weeding out, extirpation; purification (of harmful elements)

بیستن   bɪstĭn = bistĭn   to hear

بیاره   bɪyaré   Biyara (a small town in Sul. Liwa near Iranian border)

بیاره یی   bɪyaréí   inhabitant of Biyara

bl- see bĭl-

بلاو = بیلاو   bl̲aw = bĭláw   widespread

بلیسه   bl̲esé   flame

بـــو   bo¹   to (person or place). ʔəyda --- tó he is giving it to you. ba bčin --- sərčnár let's go to Serchinar. Purpose: ʔəřwa bo nanxwardĭn he's going (in order) to eat. for, in the interest of. ʔəykəm bo tó I'm doing it for you. --- yəkém jar for the first time. -´-yə that is why... --- ʔəwé-i (foll. by subjunct.) in order that...

بـــو   bó² = bóči   why? -´- ʔəwəndə xopərĭstĭn why are you so selfish? ʔədéb -´-yə pəyda buwə kə... the reason literature has come into being is for it to...

بو چی   bóči?   why?

بوجه ، بودجه   bojé   budget

بولـــه   bol̲é   grumbling (n.)

بو مبا   bombá   bomb

بو مبای   bombáy   Bᴐmbay

بـــون   bon   perfume, scent, fragrance; smell. --- le hatĭn to smell of; to suggest. --- k. to smell, sniff at s.th. bonyan náka he won't sniff at them. --- lə xoy d. to wear, put on perfume. bon lə xóm ʔədəm I wear perfume

بەبوندی   boné: bə-́-i ...(əwə) on the occasion of. bə ---i ʔə́mjəžnə̀wə on the occasion of this festival

بون وبەرامه   bonubəramé scent; perfume

بــور   bor a beating. --- d. to beat (in a game). -́-i dam he beat me. --- xwardĭn to be beaten, lose (a game)

بورجوازیەت   bòrjwazɪyét bourgeoisie

بــوش   boš empty

بویاغ   boyáγ a shine. --- k. to shine (shoes)

بویاغچی   boyaγčí bootblack

بویاخ   boyáx paint; polish

بویه   boyé paint. --- k. to paint s.th.

بوینباغ   boɲbáγ necktie

بوزانین   bozanín advertisement, notice

بر   br- see bĭr-

بوه   buwé rich; rich man

بووك   buk bride

بوکەشوشه   bukəšušé doll; toys

بوم   bum earth

بوومەلەرزه   bùmələrzé earthquake

بـــوون   bún[1] (past stem: bu-; present: copula suffix, sg. 1 -ĭm/m, 2 -it/-yt, 3 -ə/-yə [-eti after pron. suff. -y]; pl. 1 -in/ -yn, 2 -ĭn/-n, 3 -ĭn/-n = present time 'is, are, am'; stem b- = future time or subjunctive) to be. dĭréɳ bu it was late. dréɳə it is late. žĭɲyeti she is his wife. čóni? how are you? čón ʔəbi? how will you be? xóti is that you? həžár ʔemə̀yn the poor are we. nábe nəxóš bĭbi you mustn't be sick. dyar nít you are not to be seen! where

have you been? to exist. kəwatà hər
níyə then it does not exist at all!
kə́sman lə máləwə nabet no one will be
home. ʔemə́ čwár kəs buyn we were four
people (there were four of us.). Also
in the sense of "to exist": həm, həyt,
həyə; həyn, hən, hən. ʔemə́š həyn! we
too exist! to happen, occur, take place.
čí ʔəbe? what will happen? ʔəbe[t]
(foll. by subjunct.) must, ought to,
should. --- bř̌om I must go. --- ř̌oyš-
tỉbet he must have left, he must be
gone. --- baštỉr fəri bỉn you should learn
it better. ʔəbu (foll. by subjunct.) it
was necessary, ought to have, should have.
--- hər ʔə́wsatè ř̌a bwəstayə It simply
should have stopped. nábe must not.
--- bř̌oy you mustn't go. ʔaxỉr ---
come now, that won't do. wə nə́be (foll.
by subjunct.) is not something that...
wa nə́bu (foll. by subjunct.) the situation was not such that... ʔəw nə́be if
it were not for that; otherwise. ʔéwə
bỉnu xwa I entreat you, I beg of you.
boy bun kə (foll. by subjunct.) to have
the right, option, power to (do s.th.).
---yan həyə kə bínernəwə they have the
right to send it back. lə (inf.) da ---
to be in the process of, be ---ing. lə
zorbúŋdayə it is increasing. lə nan-
xwardỉnayn we are eating. lə...bə dər
--- to be devoid of, be lacking in...
ləgəl̠...y --- to be talking to, address-
ing s.o. ləgə́l̠ mỉntə are you talking to
me? wə̀ku hər ləgəl̠ ʔə́wišyan nə́be as if
they were not even talking to him. pewə
--- to have with (it), be accompanied by;
to be on s.th. pəyda --- lə...əwə, lə...
pəyda --- to come out of, originate from.
pəydabúwə originated; created. --- bə
to become; to turn into, be transformed
into. kə́ bu bə sərək wəzirán? who became president? bù bə səɾat də́ it became 10:00, it turned 10:00. --- bə yək
to be united, unite. búnə to become.

بــــوون   bún² existence. nəbún non-existence

بـــوونهوه   bunəwə́ (b-) to recur; to become.
nə́betəwə (which) will not happen again;

unequaled, superb. lə...--- to be finished with s.th.

بوقله مون   buqləmín a turkey

بوژاند نه وه   bužandnəwé[1] (bužen-) to revive

بوژاند نه وه   bužandnəwé[2] revivification

بوژانه وه   bužanəwé (buže-) to live again

بو گله   buglé artificial curl. --- bə sér the
one with the curl (in his hair), "curly-
locks"

بوردن   burdín (bur-), lə...--- to forgive s.o.
bïmbúrə pardon me!

له خو بوردن   lə xoy burdín to surrender o.s.; to sacrifice o.s.

برج   burj tower

را بواردن   bwardín (bwer-): řa --- to pass time.
xóšman řa bward we had a nice time

بویـــژ   bwež poet

č

چـــای   ča, čay tea. ---yan xwardəwə they
drank tea. čám bo bènə bring me some
tea

چابـز   čabéz teapot

چـادر   čadïr tent

چـاك   čak good; well (not sick). čóni? čaki
škur? how are you--well, I hope? ---
b.əwə to get well, recover. --- k. to
improve s.th.; to set (a watch). ---
k.əwé to repair, mend; to cure. ---
lə...k. bə láda to buckle down to s.th.

چاك بونه وه   čakbunəwé recovery

چاكـ   čaké goodness; good action; advantage

33

چاکه‌ت	čakét jacket, coat
چاك كردن	čakkïrdín improvement
چالاك	čalák shrewd; active; nimble; prompt
چال	čal̲ hole, pit; deep
چاندن	čandín (čen-) to sow
چاپ	čap printing press. --- k. to print, publish. --- nékraw unpublished
چار	čar relief; help. --- k. to remedy, cure. tazə ---i nákret can no longer be cured
چاره	čaré¹ face; countenance; appearance
چارة	čaré² remedy, cure. be --- distressed. --- k. to remedy, cure. čón ---i ʔém dardə bkəyn? how shall we remedy this ill?
چاره‌ك	čarék quarter, one-fourth. bə --- səʕátek in a quarter of an hour
چاره‌ كردن	čarəkïrdín solving, remedying (n.); treatment
چاره‌ نووس	čarənús destiny, fate, lot; predestination
چاره‌ سه‌ر	čarəsər remedy, cure. --- k. to remedy, correct (an ill)
چاره‌ سه‌ر كردن	čarəsərkïrdín solving, remedying (n.)
چاروكه	čaroké apron
چاو	čaw eye. bém --- ə̀ from this perspective. bə --- compared to, in comparison with. sər --- at your service! mə̀rhəhə sər --- hello! (in response; enthusiastic). --- bïřín (bř-) to eye s.th. avidly. --- k.əwə to open one's eyes; to keep one's eyes open, be careful. ---y bə...gerán (ger-) to look, glance at. ---y bə...kəwtín to catch sight of; to see; ---ək bə...da xïšandín (xšen-) to

cast a glance over, survey. ---y lə...b.
to see, look at. --- tewə b. to look
after. ---yan ləwéyə kə... they have
their eyes on, they have hopes of...
--- lə...k. to imitate. --- řun b.ewə
to be pleased by. ...y bər čaw kəwtı́n
to come into view; to catch sight of...
lə --- wun b. to disappear from view.
ləbər --- b. to be before the eye; to
be clear, apparent. --- bı̌řínə --- to
look s.o. in the eye, look in s.o.'s
face. henánə bər --- to bring to mind.
xı̌stnə bər --- (xə-) to display, show.
xı̌stnə peš --- to put before one's eyes;
to present

چاوبرسی   čawbı̌rsí greedy, niggardly

چاوبەست   čawbést deception. --- k. lə to deceive
s.o.

چاودیری   čawderí supervision. --- k. to guard,
protect, take care of

چاوەری کردن   čawəřé k. to wait for, to anticipate

چاوەروان   čawəřwán expectation. ---i...b. to
expect, wait for, anticipate; to look
forward to. ---i...k. to expect, wait
for. ---i ʔəwə nákən kə... they do not
expect that...

چاوگیران   čawgerán a glance at (bə)

چاویلکه   čawilké eyeglasses, spectacles

چاووبرو   čawubı̌ró eyes and eyebrows

چاخانه   čaxané = čayxané teashop

چای   čay = ča (čay is not used with pron.
suff.) tea

چایچی   čayčí teashopkeeper. dərwíš šəríf-i
--- Dərwish Sharif the teashopkeeper

چایخانه   čayxané teahouse

چیشت   češt food, viands. --- le nán (ne-)
to prepare a meal.

35

چیشته نگاو	češtəŋáw, češthəŋáw noon
چیشتن	češtín (čež-) to taste (food, etc.) cf. čištín
چیشتکەر	češtkér cook
چــیو	čew rib
چــیز	čež taste; savory
چه ··· چه	čə...čə whether...or. see čĭ...čĭ
چه فته	čəfté a piece of silk fabric used as a headdress
چه ك	čək[1] arms; weapon
چه ك دان له	čək[2] lə...da dán to kneel, squat down on...
چه ك به د ه ست	čəkbədést, čəkbədés armed person; fighter; soldier
چه کمه	čəkmé boots
چه کمه بور	čəkməbór soldier
چه م	čəm stream, brook, river
چه ماندن	čəmandín (čəmen-) to curve, bend s.th.
چه مه ن	čəmén = čimén lawn
چه مه ر	čəmér funeral
چه مین	čəmín (čəm-) to bend (intr.)
چه ناگه	čənagé chin
چه نــد	čənd (interrog.) how much? -´- pyaw how many men? lém --- anèda in the past few days, of late, recently. Exclamation: how much! how great! how...! --- tĭrs-i ʔémsərdanèy lə díl bu what great fear she had of this visit! --- kíček-i ziréki what a clever girl you are! -´-...ek some, several, a few. -´- pyawek a few men

چه نـدى   čəndí   quantity

چه نه دان   čənə d. to prattle, chatter. ---i čí
ʔəda what is he chattering about?

چه نه باز   čənəbáz talkative; chatterbox. to
kïček-i ---i you're a talkative girl

راچه نین   čənín: řa --- (čən-) to wake up with a
start

چه پ   čəp left hand

چه په   čəpə́ left (adj.); left-handed

چه په ل   čəpél dirty, filthy

چه پله   čəplə́ clap, clapping. --- le d. to
clap

چه پوك   čəpók slap. --- kešan bə sər-i... (keš-)
to slap s.o. on the head (in disapproval)

چه پوراست   čəpuřást left hand and right hand

چه پوراسته   čəpuřasté ambidextrous

چه ق   čəq middle, center; stick. ---i řegá
the middle of the street (leading no-
where)

چه قانـدن   čəqandín (čəqən-) to plant

چه قه ل   čəqél jackel

چه قین   čəqín (čəq-) to stick into; to be
planted; to ram

چه قـو   čəqó knife

چه توكه ر   čəqokér cutler, knife-maker

چه رم   čərm tough leather; skin

چه رمه سه رى   čərməsərí trouble; suffering

چه رخ   čérx[1] era, epoch, age; century. ---i
pášu péš mežu historic and pre-historic
times

چه رخ	čərx² wheel; machine
چه رخ	čərx³ cigarette lighter
چه رخاندن	čərxandín (čərxen-) to cause s.th. to rotate. wər --- to change, reverse s.th.
چه رخين	čərxín (čərx-) to rotate, roll, revolve (intr.)
چه رخوفه له گ	čərxufəlég a swing
چه ش	čéš taste (in art, etc.)
چه شم ئه نذازی	čə̀šimʔəndazí scene, view
چه شن	čéšin manner; way, fashion, manner. bém ---ə̀ in this manner. lə čənd --- of various kinds. čə̀šnawčéšn assorted, of all kinds, manifold
چه ته	čətə́ highwayman, bandit
چه تر	čətír umbrella
چه و	čəw gravel
چه وه نده ر	čəwəndér beet
چه وساندنه وه	čəwsandnəwé oppression, persecution
چه وساو	čəwsáw distressed
چه وت	čəwt crooked; devious
چه ووز	čəwúz k. to oil, smear, annoint
چه خماخه	čəxmaxé sparks, lightening (n.)
چه خماخ ساز	čəxmaxsáz weaponsmith, gunsmith
چه خماخ سازی	čəxmaxsazí gunsmithery
چسی	čí what? ʔəwə -́-tə what's the matter (with you)? -́-tan bo bígerməwə! what a tale I have to tell you! ...y lə --- da b. how is...? how is...getting along? komələké́tan lə -́- dayə how is it going with your group?

38

چیمه ن   čimén, čəmén grass; lawn. fərš-i ---
řá xra a carpet of grass was spread out

چیمنتو   čimïntó cement

چین   čin¹ class; category; group

چین   čin² China. ---i millí Chinese People's
Republic

چیروك   čirók story, tale. kurtə --- short
story. --- gerannəwé to tell a story
(to: bo)

چه   čï- what (used attributively). čïqazánj
ʔəkəyn what profit will we derive (if...).
čïkaréy what work do you do? čï...ek
what, which. čïtəméneki what age are
you? how old are you? čïktəbekït ʔəwə
what book do you want? ta čïřadəyek to
what degree. -́-...(wə)-́- whether...
or... --- karbədəstán --- komél whether
govt. officials or private citizens

چــك   čïk rare. čïkek a little

چــل   čïl forty

چــله   čïlé the fortieth day

دا چله كاندن   čïləkandín (čləken-): da --- to startle
s.o.

دا چله كین   čïləkín (člək-): da ---, řa --- to
start, be startled

چلــــم   čïlém fortieth

چــل   čïḻ branch

چــلك   čïḻík dirt

چلــكاو   čïḻkáw impure water

چلــكاوخور   čïḻkawxór parasite

چــلكن   čïḻkín dirty

چنــار   čïnár poplar

39

چنین	čɪnín (čn-) to knit, weave
چنینه‌وه	čɪninəwé (čn-) to pick up, gather
چنگ	čɪŋ claw; paw. --- kəwtɪ́n to earn, get
چرا	čɪrá lamp. --- yek-i řunak-i šəfqədár bu he was a bright and shining light
چرچ	čɪrč creased; wrinkled
چریکاندن	čɪrikandɪ́n (čɪriken-) to shriek, scream
چریسکه	čɪriské chirp
چرو ، چروو	čɪró, čɪrú branches; shoots
چرپاندن	čɪrpandɪ́n (čɪrpen-) to whisper. bə gwéyda méčɪrénə don't whisper in his ear!
چرپ چرپ	čɪrpəčɪ́rp whispering (n.). kə --- pəydá bu when whispering began, when people began to whisper. --- k. to whisper
چرر	čɪř dense, thickly-wooded
چررنووك	čɪřnúk claw
چشتن	čɪštɪ́n, čežán (čež-) to taste s.th.; to experience (hardships, etc.) cf. češtɪ́n. ʔəw həmíʔazaranəm čɪšt I have suffered all of those pains
چیا	čɪyá mountain
چوك	čok (da) d. to kneel
چوله‌که	čoləké sparrow. zmàn-i ---əkéy xwarduwə he chatters like a parrot
چول	čoḻ vacant; desert. --- k. to vacate (a place)
چولی	čoḻí emptiness
چون	čon how? ---ɪt zani how did you find out? how can...? why...? --- názane? how can he not know?! how, as, just as.

40

‑‑‑ït diwin hər wayn we are just as you
(last) saw us. hər‑‑‑ə(k)bu be that as
it may, at any rate, in any case

چونیەتى   čonetí method, manner, way; how to (do
s.th.); quality; state

چــونى   coní quality

چــوپى   čopí dancing (n.)

چــورون   čun (č‑; imperat. ‑čo‑) to go (to a
place, to do s.th.,(as opp. to řoyštin
to go away, leave). ʔəčím bó bazàr, ʔəčmə
bazár I'm going to the market-place.
ču bo kwé where did he go? bə dəŋəkéwə
čum I went toward the voices. bəsər
‑‑‑ to go away, depart. dər ‑‑‑ to
come out, appear; to be published. řəs-
məkán báš dər čun the pictures came out
well. ʔotombìlek-i nwé dər čuwə a new
car has come out. čéŋ řožname dèr ʔəču?
how many newspapers used to be published?
bo dər ‑‑‑ to escape; to sneak out. dər
‑‑‑ lə to succeed in s.th. ʔəbé ʔımsal
dér čïn lə məktəb you must succeed iñ
school this year (i.e., be promoted).
həl ‑‑‑ to jump over. la ‑‑‑ to go
awāy. lá čo! get out of here! lə...
‑‑‑ to look like, resemble. lə báwki
ʔəče he looks like his father. pe ‑‑‑
to take (time). zóri pe nəču he did not
take long (before...), without delay
he... řa ‑‑‑ to leak, go out. te həl
‑‑‑ to start, get started (doing s.th.).
tek‑‑‑ to stir; to change; to lose one's
composure; to be unsettled, disturbed,
"go to pieces." bəbé ʔəwə-i kəmızór tek
bìčet without losing her self-control in
the least. lə...tek ‑‑‑ to mistake s.o.
tek ‑‑‑ ləgəl...da to disagree with.
mìn ték čum ləgélya I disagreed with him.
‑‑‑ə péšəwə to march forward, advance,
progress. ‑‑‑ə sér to descend upon,
attack

چونەوه   čunəwé (č‑) to fade (: color)

چونکه   čúŋkə, čúŋki because

41

چوالە	čwalə́ green almond
چوار	čwar four
چوار چیوە	čwarčewə́, čawčə́w frame
چواردە	čwardə́ fourteen
چوار مەشقی	čwarməšqí cross-legged
چواری	čwarpə́ quadruped, esp. donkey
چوارشەمە	čwaršəmmə́ Wednesday. řož-i --- Wednesday
چوارتا	čwartá Chwarta (place name)
چیا	čya mountain

d

دا	da (preverb, a particle used only in verbal phrases where it is usually stressed; verbal phrases are listed under the verb or, if any, noun or adj. included in the phrase) down. da nə́n to place, put down; to install (a machine). cf. nə́n to put, place. ləwe dáy nə place it down over there. It is often difficult to determine the meaning of da: dán to give; da dán to sharpen (a pencil).
دائما	daʔimə́n = dáyma always
دائــرە	daʔirə́ = dayərə́ office, government office
دابەستە	dabəstə́ fattened lamb
دابەش	dabə́š k. bəsər...(da) to distribute s.th. to
دابەشکردن	dabəškïrdín distribution
داد	dad justice
دادگا	dadgá court

داده مند   dadménd   just, fair

داگــير   dagir k.   to invade; to conquer

داگــيركەر   dagirkér   invader

داگيركردن   dagirkïrdïn   invasion. jegá --- invasion area; military base

داك   dak = dayk   mother

دال   dal̲   raven; kite (bird)

دالان   dal̲án   vestibule

دامه   damé   checker, draught

دامغه   damɣé   seal

دامودەزگا   damʋdəzgá   set up; means

دان   dán¹   tooth

دان   dan²   grain; seed

دان به خودا گرتن   dan³: --- bə xoyda gïrtïn to collect o.s., regain one's composure

دان نــان به   dan⁴: --- bə...nán (ne-) to acknowledge, recognize (a country); to confess

دان   dan⁵: (də-; pass. dr-) to give, grant. ʔəydəm bə tó I'll give it to you. náməwe br̆om hətaku parə nédəm bə ʔewé I don't want to go until I have given the money to you. méydə bə kə̀s don't give it to anyone. bər...--- to hurl...at s.o.; to beat, pelt s.o. with s.th. da --- to put s.th. down; to rest (the elbow, etc.); to cut, sharpen (pencil). həl̲ --- to interrupt. həl̲ -́-e to speak in behalf of, lend support to s.o. lə...--- to touch; to hit, strike; to play (a musical instrument). bə dést lèm da I touched it with my hand. to cud le ʔədəyt? do you play the lute? lə čí ʔədəyt what do you play? le -́- r̃uwəw to repair to; hear for. lə...həl̲ --- to kick. ...lə ...həl̲ -́- to defend s.o. against s.th. šəq lə̄ mïn həl̲ nádən they do not protect

me from the kicking. ləsər...həl ---
to intervene on behalf of, come to the
support of. ləséri həl nádən they do
not rally to its help. řa --- to sweep
away, push aside. te həl --- to kick,
beat s.o. up. tek --- to destroy; to
dissolve; to displace, disarrange; to
take apart; to confuse, upset, disturb.
tek wər --- to shake s.th. dáne to
give s.th. to s.o. dináreki̇̆t ʔədəyne we'll
give you a dinar. bi̇̆mdəre give it to me!
--- bəsər to cover s.o. with

دانـــا daná wise; tact

دانـــه danə́¹ one piece; one copy; item; a unit
(of)

دانـــه danə́² grain

دانـــهر danə́r writing(s)

دانـــهش danə́š knowledge, learning, lore

دانـــهوه danəwə́ (də-) to give back, repay. həl
--- to uncover. pəčəkéy həl dáyəwə
she took her veil off. lek --- to de-
liberate, study (a matter); to interpret
s.th. (as: bə). léki dayəwə she pon-
dered it over. bə šúm bo xóyan lek
dáyəwə they interpreted it as an evil
omen for themselves

دانیشتگا daništgá, danišgá university

دانشتوو ، دانشتوان daništú seated; residing; pl.: residents,
inhabitants; population

دان نان به dannán bə...da admission, acknowledge-
ment of

دانسـاز dansáz dentist

دانـــووله danulə́ boiled wheat

داپیر dapír grandson

دار dár tree; wood, piece of wood; fire-
wood

دارا   dará   rich; Dara (m.p.n.)

دارايـــى   daraí   wealth

دارچین   darčín   cinnamon

داردەست   dardést   cane, stick; staff

دارەبەن   darəbén   terebrinth, turpentine trees

دارەتەرم   darətérm   a wooden frame for carrying the dead to the cemetery; coffin

دارستان   darïstán   forest

دارۆخان   daroxán   Darokhan (a village in Sulaimania Liwa)

دارپەروەر   darpərwér   tree-lover

دارتاش   dartáš   carpenter

دارتاشی   dartaší   carpentry

داروردەخت   darudréxt   trees and plants

داروپەردو   darupərdú   debris, rubble

داررو   dařú   arsenic

داس   das   scythe, sickle

داستان   dastán   tale, story

داو   daw   net, snare

داوا   dawá   demand; request. --- k. to ask; to demand; to ask the hand of. --- lə... k. (kə foll. by subjunct.) to ask of s.o. (that he do s.th.)

داواکـــردن   dawakïrdín   demand; request

داوەن   dawén   foot of a mountain

داخ   dax   sorrow, sadness, grief. dax! (exclam. of grief) oh! dáxəkəm alas! ---i gránïm how great is my sorrow! bə ---əwe sorrowfully. zór bə ---əwe ʔələyn we are very sad to say... ---ïm

45

náče bo səgəkét my sorrow for your [deceased] dog does not cease. --- xwardǐn (xo-) to become sad

داخوشی daxoší joy. --- d.əwə to console, soothe

داخوراو daxuráw squinting, askance; frightening (:eyes)

داخوازی dàxwazí demand, request

دایهك dayə́k foster-mother

دایهره dayərə́, daʔirə́ office

داییك dayík, dayk mother. lə --- b. to be born. lə --- kəwtnə xwarəwə to be born

دایکسی daykí motherhood

دایما dáyma, dáʔima always

دی de (pl. dehát) village

دیهساتی dehatí relating to villages

دیل del̲ bitch

له دیر زمانهوه der: lə -́- zəmanəwə from time immemorial

دیر deř line (on a page)

دیسو déw demon

دیسوودرنج dewudǐrǐnj devils and demons

دیم dem, deyn, déynəwə, etc., dial var. of، yem, yeyn, yéynəwə (pres. tense of hatǐn to come)

ده də¹ ten. --- pənjá ten or fifteen

ده də² (asseverative part. preceding imperative or implied imperatives). -́- bro go on! --- bášə that's enough! stop it! cf. dəy

ده də-³ dial. var. Sul. ʔə-, prefix of imperfective aspect

46

دەبو   dəbó   ammunition storage point and a place for training recruits; barracks

دەفتەر   dəftér   notebook

دەگمەن   dəgmén : bə --- rarely, seldom, hardly ever

دەهـول   dəhól   drum

دەم   dəm¹ mouth. bər --- in the face of, before. bəsər -́-a face down. lə ---...da immediately behind. ---i xən jér blade of a dagger. --- k.əwé to open one's mouth; to speak. ǧirtin bə ---əwə to repeat constantly, keep talking about

دەم   dəm² period, time. ləm ---ə-i ʔaxriyéda in the recent past. -́-e a long time. -́-ekə it has been a long time now that... -́-ekbu (it had been) for a long time. bə ---...əwə while (doing s.th.) bə --- řoyštnéwə while walking

دەمانچه   dəmančé pistol

دەمـار   dəmár vein; nerve. ša --- the largest blood vessel, the vital vein or nerve

دەمارکرژ   dəmarkírž arrogant

دەمبوس   dəmbús a straight pin

دەمه   dəmé time, period

دەم و چاو   dəmučáw face

دەمەتەقی   dəmətəqé chat, idle conversation

دەنگ   déŋ voice; noise, sound. --- lə kərənáwə həsta a sound came out of the horn. --- d.əwé to reverberate, echo

دەنگەدەنگ   dəŋədéŋ noise. givém lə -́-ə I hear noise

دەنك   dəŋk pebble

47

دەنکوباس	dəŋubás information, data. --- wər-gĭrtín the collection of information
دەنکوسەنگ	dəŋusáŋ noise, sound. híc ---ek no sound at all
دەقیقە	dəqiqá, dəyəqqá minute (time)
دەر	dár out; outside. lə... bə --- nıyə is not devoid of... see also dárəwə 'outside'
دەربار	dərbár court
دەربارەی	dərbará-i about, concerning
دەربەدەر کردن	dərbədàr k. to eject (from home, country, etc.); to cast out; displacement, rendering homeless
دەربەندی خان	dərbànd-i xán Derbendi Khan (pl. n., Sul. Liwa)
دەرچون	dərčún publication; implementation
دەرد	dárd ailment, ill; sickness, disease
دەردەسەری	dàrdəsərí pains; invonveniences; diffi-culties
دەرەبەگ	dərəbág feudal lord
دەرەبەگی	dərəbəgí feudalism
دەرەج	dəréj, dərəjá degree. ---i hərará tem-perature
دەرەجە	dərəjá degree (temperature); grade, mark (in school)
دەرقەت هاتن	dərəqət hatín (ye-) to be able to (over-power s.o.)
دەرەوە	dárəwə out, outside; abroad. bó néhatitə ---? why didn't you come out(side)? bə --- b. to be outside; to be exposed to view
دەرگا	dərgá door. ---i dárəwə the outside door

ده رهینان	dərhenán removal, extracting, pulling out (n.)
ده رحال	dərhál immediately
ده ركی سه را	dərk: ---i sərá gate of government build-ing. bər ---i sərá the space in front of a government building
ده ركه وتن	dərkəwtín advent, appearance
ده رمان	dərmán medicine
ده رمانخوارد	dərmanxwárd poison
ده رپه رین	dərpəřín ejection, blasting forth (n.)
ده رس	dərs ḷesson; subject (in school). --- xwendín (xwen-) to study
ده رسخواندن	dᵉrsxwendín studying (n.), studies
ده روون	dərún insides, innards; innermost part; conscience, mind
ده روازه	dərwazə́ portal, large door
ده رخستن	dərxïstín expression (of opinions)
ده رزی	dərzí needle
ده س	dəs = dəst --- k. bə to get started on s.th.
ده سدریژی	dəsdreží aggression; interference. --- k. to interfere
ده ستەلات	dəsəḷát, dəstəḷát authority, power
ده ستەسر	dəsəsír, dəstəsír handkerchief
ده سگا	dəsgá = dəzgá establishment; organi-zation
ده سگیربوون	dəsgir bún to find, discover; to secure, obtain, get
ده ست	dəst hand. dᵉstīt xošbe blessed be your hand! God bless you! (an expression of thanks for a favor or a service ren-dered). ---bəjə́ soon; immediately. bə -́-́ powerful. lə --- čun to slip out

of the hand, be lost. --- d. bə qəlóm
to take pen in hand. déstyan dawətə̄ qə-
lému ləsər ʔəmbasə̀ ʔənusĭn they take
[took] pen in hand and write on this subject. bo...--- d. to be useful, suitable
for... lə --- d., lə dəzdán to miss,
not to avail o.s. of s.th. --- g. to
bear, carry (arms, weapon etc.). --- g.
bə...əwə to hold on to...with one's
hands; to cover...with one's hands. lə
--- hatĭn to be able to. --- kešán bo
šər (keš-) to reach out for ș.th.; to
grasp, seize. ...y dəst kəwtĭn to come
to the hands of; to get, obtain, earn,
win ... bo ʔəwé-i jegáyek-i bašman dəs
kəwe so that we will get a good place.
ʔəmřo dinárekĭm dəst kəwtúwə ˏI've earned
a dinar today. --- lə...xĭstĭn (xə-) to
touch s.th. ---y k. bə... to start
(doing...) (intrans.). ---yan kĭrd bə
pekənin they began to laugh. dəs kráwə
bə konkrít work has been begun on the
concrete. --- pekrá, begun, started
(participle). ---y k.ə mĭl-i... to embrace s.o. --- bə...da nán (ne-) to
press, squeeze (with the finger or hand).
d.ə --- to appoint s.o. in charge of.
wʊlat-i babáni dràyə dóst he was appoint-
ed head of the Baban nation. d.ə ---...
əwə to hand over, give s.th. to ...; to
place s.th. in the hands of, entrust
s.th. to ... həlwaké ʔədənə dèstiəwə
they hand him the candy. g.ə --- to take
s.th. in hand; to take charge of, assume
(responsibility of). ʔišukári ʔəgatə
dəst he takes over his functions

دەستدریژی	dəstdĭreží = dəsdrezí aggression, attack
دەستە	dəsté group, set; dozen. --- brakáni his brethren, his colleagues
دەستەلات	dəstəlát power; authority
دەستەپارچە	dèstəparčé helpless. --- nín kə... they are not so helpless that...
دەستەسر	dəstəsír = dəsəsír handkerchief

ده ستكار   dəstkár fashioning, creating, manufacturing (adj.)

ده ستنووس   dəstnús manuscript

ده ستودايره   dəstudayəré followers and officials

ده ستوپی   dəstupé hands and feet; limbs

ده ستوپيوند   dəstupewénd servants; retinue

ده ستور   dəstúr constitution (law); manner of behaving. bə ---i xóyan in their own way. ---i zman-i kurdí Kurdish grammar

ده شت   déšt level ground, (vast) plain; desert

ده شتايی   dəštaí level ground (as opp. to hilly)

ده وام   dəwám a long time. ---i həyə it lasts a long time. --- k. to persist

به رده وام بوون تيا   dəwám: see bərdəwam bún tya to persevere in, to continue at

ده وه ن   dəwén bush

ده وله مه ند   dəwleménd rich, wealthy

ده وله ت   dəwlét nation, state, country. dəwlə-təyəkgïrtwekán the United States

ده ور   dəwr¹ age, period. ---i bérd the Stone Age

ده وور   dəwr² rôle. --- nwandín (nwen-) to represent its rôle = to play its part (in s.th.)

ده وور   dəwr³ around. bə ---i...da around. lə ---i... around. ---i...d. to encircle. bə ---i...da hatín to show fondness for, fawn over

ده وره   dəwré: ---i...d. to encircle...

ده وری   dəwrí tournament

ده وروبه ر   dəwrubér vicinity (in time or place). lə ---i...(da) around, surrounding

ده و ر و پشت	dəwrupíšt vicinity. lə --- around, surrounding; on all sides, all around
د ه ی	déy (asseverative part., used with imperatives) də břo déy 'go on! cf. də²
د ه ست به سه ر	dəzbəsér exiled, restricted to a certain area; cf. dùrxráwətowə, exiled (abroad)
د ه ز گا ، د ه سگا	dəzgá institution, office, establishment; organization
د ه ستگیران	dəzgirán fiancée
د ه ز و و	dəzú string; thread
د ی	dí: hatnə -´- to come into existence; to materialize, be realized. henànə -´- to put into effect, implement, realize s.th.
د یل	díl captive, prisoner. ...bə --- g. to take...prisoner
د یلسی	dilí slavery, servitude, captivity
دیمه ن	dimén appearance; view, scenery. bə -´- in appearance; on the surface
دیموکراتی	dimʊkratí, dimuqratí democratic. hɪzb-i --- the Democratic Party
دیموکراتیه ت	dimʊkratɪyét, dimuqratɪyét democracy
دین	din¹ religion
دین	dín² (no pres. stem) to see. həlpəřk̀e-i lʊbnaním diwə I have seen Lebanese dance. cf. binín
دینــار	dinár dinar (Iraqi monetary unit, = U.S. $2.80)
دینه وه	dinəwé (no pres. stem) to see, see again; to find
دینــسی	diní religious, pertaining to religion
دیسانه وه	dísanəwə, dísan again, once again; also, then

ديته   díte since, as

ديتن   ditïn (no present stem) to see

ديو   díw side (of mountain, page, record, etc.). ʔém--- this side, cis-. ʔéw --- that side, trans-. léw---əwə on the other side. wəře ʔém --- come this way

ديوار   diwár wall

ديوەخانه   diwəxané visitors' room

ديزه   dizé, dim. dizəlé, dizəloké water jar

دل   dïl heart. --- ʔawenə-i -́-ə one heart is the mirror of the other one ("the feelings are mutual") (prov.). lə ---i xóma within myself. bə -́- enthusiastic; earnest; with all one's heart, wholeheartedly, warmly. bə ---ek-i pák with good will. bə ---y b. to be to one's taste, to like. bə dïlmə it's to my taste, I like it. dʊdïl b. lə to hesitate over. --- bə...xoš b. to be pleased with. --- bə...da čún to set one's heart on, like...---y hatïn (foll. by subjunct.) to have the heart to (do s.th.). --- k.əwə to open up one's heart; to rejoice, be delighted. ---i...šïkandïn (šken-) to rebuff...; to disappoint...

دلاوەر   dïlawér valiant

دل فرين   dïlfïrén enchanting, captivating

دلگير   dïlgír charming, captivating (things). xóẏ --- k. to distress o.s., make o.s. unhappy

دنگيرى   dïlgirí sadness, sorrow, regret

دل كەرەوه   dïlkərəwé delightful; enchanting

دل پاك   dïlpák sincere

دل پاكى   dïlpakí purity of heart, sincerity

دل نيا   dïlnɪyá assured, reassured

دلسوز   dïlsóz kind, benevolent

53

دل ته نگ	dïltéŋ	grieved, sad
دل ته نگی	dïltəŋí	distress; heartbreak
دل ته ر	dïltér	sprightly, gay
دل تر سين	dïltïrsén	fraught with fear; terrifying
دلوده رون	dïludərún	one's inner organs
دلخوش	dïlxóš	happy
دلخواز	dïlxwáz	desire
دنيـا	dïnyá, dunyá the world
دراو	dïráw	money. --- le d. to coin money
دراوه سه ر	dïrawəsér	gold coins worn on the head
دراوسی	dïrawsé	neighbor; neighboring
دريژ	dïréž	long; tall. --- da dïřín (dř-) to be talkative. --- k.əwé to lengthen; to extend (a hand)
دريژ ايی	dïrežaí	length
دريژ دادر	dïreždadíř	loquacious, talkative
دريژه کيشان	dïrežé: --- kešán (keš-) to last long
دريژی	dïreží	length
دره نگ	dïréŋ	late. bém --- wəxtè at this late hour [of the night]
دره وش	dïrəwš	awl
دره وشاند نه وه	dïrəwšandnəwé (drəwše-) to flash, sparkle
دره خت	dïréxt	trees (in general)
در نده یی	dïrïndəí	savageness
در نگ	dïrïngé	(onom.: sound produced by pounding on s.th. full or solid)
در نج	dïrïnj	devil

54

درو	dĭró lie, falsehood. --- k. to tell a lie. bə --- xĭstĭn (xə-) to belie, give the lie to
دروزن	dĭrozĭn liar
درشت	dĭršt adult
دروون	dĭrún (dru-) to sew
درونه‌وه	dĭrunəwə́ (dru-) to mow
دروست کردن	dĭrúst, dʊrúst right; well done. --- k. to make, build, construct
دروستکه‌ر	dĭrustkə́r, drustkə́r creator; creative
درووستکراو	dĭrustkráw made, manufactured. lə žapón ---ə (it is) made in Japan
دروشم	dĭrúšm symbol
درز	dĭrz crack
دڕ	dĭř raptorial; fierce
دڕاندن	dĭřandĭ́n (dřen-) to tear s.th.
دڕین	dĭřĭ́n (dř-) to tear off. da --- to rip, tear open
دڕک	dĭřĭk thorn
دڕرکودال	dĭřkudál thorns and weeds (lit., "thorns and ravens")
دش	dĭš husband's sister
دوان	dĭwán = dwan (dwe-) to speak
دز	dĭz thief
دزین	dĭzĭ́n (dĭz-) to steal
دژ	dĭž fortress
دژوار	dĭžwár problem
دژواری	dĭžwarí crisis

ديانات	dɪyanát	religion
د و	do	<u>do</u> (a sour milk drink)
د ول	do<u>l</u>	valley
دونكيشوت	donkišót	Don Quixote
دوراندن	dorandín (doren-) to lose. čɪl fɪlsɪt doránuwə you've lost 40 fils	
دوست	dost	friend
دوستایەتی	dostayətí friendship. ʔəyəwe --- ləgəl həmú gəlan-i dʊnyá bɪkat it wants to make friends with all the nations of the world	
دوش دوش	došdóš	languidly
دوشەك	došék	mattress
دوزەخ	dozéx	hell, inferno
دوزینەوه	dozinəwə́¹ (doz-) to find; to discover. ʔətdózməwə I'll find you	
دوزینەوه	dozinəwə́²	invention; discovery
د ر	dr-: see dɪr-	
د و	du two. --- jar twice. -ɪ̀- sé two or three	
دووباره	dubaré	double
دووبەرەكی	dubərəkí	hostility; dissension
دوودل بوون	dudɪl: --- b. lə... to hesitate over; to dɪstrust, lack confidence in	
دوهەم	duhém = dʊwém, duhəmín second; secondly	
دووكەوانه	dukəwané	parenthesis
دوور	dur far, far away, distant. lə dúrəwə from afar. zór --- at great length, in detail. lə...--- b. to be far (removed) from... ...--- b. lə to be...far from, be at a distance of...from. lə... ---	

kəwtnəwə́ to go away from, become separated from; to digress too far from.
--- xĭstnəwə́ lə (xə-) to keep s.o. away
from, banish s.o. from

دووربین   durbín farsighted; binoculars

دوره وپه ریز   durəwpəréz wəstán (wəst-) to remain
aloof; to be indifferent (to s.th.)

دووری   durí distance. lə durí- sĭ čĭl mətrəwə
at a distance of 30 to 40 meters

دوورودریژ   dùrudĭréž far and wide; at length, in
detail. bə --- at length, in detail.
--- ləséri ʔəʹron they go over it in
detail, they analyze it up and down

دوورخراوه ته وه   durxrawətowə́ exiled (abroad); cf. dəz-
bəsér

دوسبه ی   dúsbəy the day after tomorrow

دوشه مه   dušəmmə́ Monday

دوان   duwán (dwe-) = dwan to speak

دووم   duwə́m second

دوگمه   dugmə́ button

دوکان   dukán shop, store

دوکاندار   dukandár shopkeeper

دوکتور   duktór, duxtór physician, doctor

دنیا   dunyá, dĭnyá world. gəlàn-i --- the
nations of the world

دوشمن   dušmĭ́n, dužmĭ́n enemy

دوژمن   dužmĭ́n enemy

دوژمنایه تی   dužmĭnayətí ləgəḻ...da enmity, animosity
against

دوا   dwá (precedes modified n.) the last, the
final. --- sal the last year (of...).
bə --- da afteṟ it, in its wake. --- bə

--- immediately following, in the wake of. ləwé bə---wə from there on; thenceforth. ---i after (prep.). ---i sé řož after three days. ---i gəranəwétan lə ʔəməriká after you have returned from America. lə ---i after (prep.). ---kəwtī́n (ḵəw-) to lag behind, fall back. --- xī́stī́n (sə-) to delay, hold back; to postpone

دراهینان   dwahenán bringing s.th. to an end, termination

دوایی   dwaí last, latest. ʔə́m---yə̀, lə́m---yə̀da in the recent past, in the past few days (or weeks). --- gərà̀mə̀wə bo ʔutələ́ké then I returned to the hotel. lə ---ya afterwards, later on

دواکەوتن   dwakəwtī́n falling behind; backwardness

دواکەوتو   dwakəwtú backward

دوان   dwan, dī̆wán, duwán (dwe-) to talk, speak (about: lə). to speak (a language: bə). lə...əwə --- to speak to (a point), address o.s. to, discuss

دواندن   dwandī́n (dwen-) to converse, chat, talk

دوانزه   dwanzə́ twelve

دواروژ   dwařóž the days to come, the future

دواخستن   dwaxī́stī́n delay; causing delay (n.). bəbe --- without delay

دوینی   dwéne yesterday. lə ---wə since yesterday

دیار   dyar clear, visible, obvious; sign. --- b. to be clearly visible, be seen. wá ---ə thus, it is obvious. ---ə! of course! --- d. to show, display. --- k. to indicate, specify, point out; to make clear, clarify

دیاری   dyarí present, gift

ف   f

فانيلـه   fanilé flannel

فارسى   farsí Persian (language)

فاصوليا   fasolyá beans

فيل   fél trick(s), trickery

فينك   feník cool

فــير   fer acquainted (with). ---i...b. to
learn... lə kwé ---i kʋrdí buy where
did you learn Kurdish? lə paš·ʔəwə ---
búbu now that she had learned what it
was. --- k. to teach s.o. s.th. ---i
ʕərəbím kïrdïn I taught them Arabic

فەقير   fəqír poor, penniless

فەرەح   fəréh¹ wide, roomy, spacious

فــرح   fərəh² Farah (f.p.n.)

فەرەج   fəréj Faraj (m.p.n.)

فرنسا ، فرنسه   fərənsá France

فەرهەنگ   dərhéŋ dictionary

فەرمان   fərmán order, command; decree

فەرمانبەر   fərmanbér official (govt.); civil servant

فەرمانداری   fərmandarí governorship, rule

فەرمانرەوایى   fərmanrəwaí governorship, rule, sover-
eignty

فەرمانرەوايەتى   fərmanrəwayətí rule, government; reign

فەرموده   fərmʋdə statement (honorific)

فەرمون   fərmún (fərmu-) to say (honorific) Imperative: a polite invitation: please!
fərmʋ dánišə please be seated

فرش	fərš	carpet
بی فه رری	féři: be ---	uselessness, disadvantage; damage, harm
فه وتاندن	fəwtandîn¹ (fəwten-)	to destroy; to annihilate
فه وتاندن	fəwtandîn²	complete destruction, annihilation
فه یلی	fəylí	Feyli
فضیلت	fəzilét	reverend (religious title applied to Islamic scholars)
فیل	fil	elephant. bə pe-i --- a great deal
فـیرو	firó	free, gratis. bə --- free, without cost; with impunity. bə --- d. to waste
فیشه که شیته	fišəkəšeté	(pyrotechnic) rocket
فیز	fíz	snobbishness, superciliousness
فیزیا	fizyá	physics
فداکاری	fîdakarí	(self-)sacrifice
فکرین	fîkrín (fîkr-): te --- lə řu-i...əwə to think about, have an opinion on
فلس	fîlìs	fils (1/1000 of an Iraqi dinar, about 1/3 cent)
فراوان	fîrawán	wide and spacious; broad
فریواندن	fîriwandîn (friwen-): həl --- to cheat, deceive s.o.
فرمیسك	fîrmésk	tear
فرته فرته	fîrtəfîrtə	fluttering
فرری دان	fîřé: ... --- d. to throw s.th. away. --- danə... to throw s.th. into. ---yan damə kolán they tossed me into the street
فرروکه	fîřoké	airplane

60

فروكه خانه   fï̆řokəxanə́   airport

فروفيل   fï̆řufél̲   treachery, deception

فتـوا   fï̆twá   fatwa (formal legal opinion given by Muslim religious expert). --- d. to issue a fatwa; to give a legal opinion

فرقــه   fɪrqə́   division, regiment (mil.)

فــر   fr-: see also fï̆r-

فروشتن   froštï̆n   to sell

فـــو و   fú   breath

فــؤاد   fuʔád   Fuad (m.p.n.)

فورسه ت   fʊrsə́t   vacation

فوتبول   fʊtból̲   football; soccer

ک   g

كالته   galtə́   joke. be --- ! no kidding! --- pe̅k. to sneer at, mock, make fun of

كالته چى   gal̲təčí   a butt of ridicule, a laughing-stock

كالته پى كردن   gal̲təpekï̆rdí̄n (bə...) ridiculing, laugh-ing̅ (at...) (n.)

كازه راى پشت   gazəra-i pï̆št   the middle part of the back

كيــلاس   gelás   cherry

كيم   gém   game

كيران   geřán¹ (geře-)   to take s.o. around

كيرران   geřán² (gï̆ř-)   to make, give, have (a party). ʔahə́ŋekyan geřa they had a party

كيرانـه و   geřanəwə́¹(geře-)   to tell, relate (a story). čirókekï̆t bo ʔəgereməwə I'll

61

tell you a story

گێرانـەوه   geřanəwə́[2] re̋counting, relating, telling (n.)

کەچ   gə́č gypsum

کەل   gəl[1] (pl. gəlán) people, nation. ---i kʊrd the Kurdish people. ---áni jihán the nations of the world

کەل   gəl[2] : gə́le; gə́lek lə a lot of, many. gə́lekyan hatín many of them came. gə́le jar many times, often

کەلــی   gə́le, gə́lek: see gəl[2] many, a lot of

کەلا   gəlá leaf

کەلا ریزان   gəlarezán autumnal falling of leaves; Gelarezan (name of a Kurdish month)

کەنم   gəním wheat

کەنم رەنگ   gənimře̋ŋ wheat-colored; brown-skinned, brunette

کەنج   gənj young. ʔafrə̀ktek-i --- a young woman. ---i ʔəmšarə́n you are the youth of this city

کەنمە سامی   gənmə śamí maize

کەر   gər dial. var. ʔə́gər if. --- bétu (foll. by subjunct.) in the event that, if

کەردن   gərdín neck

کەردنکەش   gərdĭnkə́š threatening; obstinate

کەرم   gərm hot

کەرما   gərmá heat. ʔəm gərmá čənd dəwam ʔəka? How long will this heat last? -́-mə I'm hot. ---t nı́yə aren't you hot?

کەرمە   gərmə́ the peak of activity; high spot, climax

کەرمی   gərmí warmth. bə --- warmly; ardently

که روك	gərók great traveler; globetrotter
که ردان	gəřán¹ (gəře-) to stroll, go for a stroll; to search
که ران	gəřán² walk, stroll; drive; excursion, pleasure trip
هه لگه ردان	gəřán³ (gəře-) həl --- to be changed, transformed. sur gəřáw reddish. zərd gəřáw yellowish; pale, pallid
هه لگه رداند ن	gəřandín (gəře-): həl --- to turn up; to change s.th. to...
که رانه وه	gəřanəwə́¹ (gəře-) to return, come back, go back; go back and forth. bə ʔutumbilə-kéman gəřaynəwə we came back in our car. bə ləndénəwə ʔəgəřeynəwə we'll return via London. --- bo, --- sər to go back to; to be ascribed, attributed to, date back to. --- dwáwə to come back; to arrive back
که رانه وه	gəřanəwə́² going back and forth (n.)
که ره ك	gəřék quarter (of town)
که ش	gəš very bright; glittering; bright (colors)
که شانه وه	gəšanəwə́ (gəše-) to blossom, open up like a flower
که شه	gəšə́ k. to grow (intr.)
که شت	gəšt journey, trip, tour
که وج	gəwj stupid
که وره	gəwrə́ big, large, great; head, chief; high-ranking, senior (official). gəwrém (voc.) sir! gəwrə̀ gəwrə́ very large. --- b. to grow up, reach adulthood. --- k. to make s.th. big, bigger, to enlarge; to honor s.o.
که وره یی	gəwrəí greatness. xwa lə --́-tan kəm nékatəwə may God not diminish you as our master

gəyandín (gəyen-) to cause s.o., s.th. to arrive; to bring, take. to convey s.th. (to: bə); to acquire s.th. (for: bə). to give to understand, make it clear (that: kə). ʔəmə wá ʔəgəyenet this gives to understand. dwa həwál way gəyand kə the last piece of news made it clear that... pe --- to tend (a plant, etc.) to maturity; to grow, cultivate s.th. (to maturity). řa --- to impart, give to understand. te --- to explain s.th. to s.o.; to apprise, inform s.o. about. ---ə to cause to arrive, to take or bring, convey s.o. or s.th. to. xóy ʔəgəyenètə bər čaxanəkə̀ he betakes himself to the front of the teashop

كەيين gəyín (gə-) = te gəyštín to come to know about, understand

كەيشتن gəyštín (gə-) to arrive; to reach, extend to; to happen, occur. bə...---, --- bə...(əwə) to arrive at; to reach (destination); to attain, obtain, achieve (an aim). ---ə to arrive at, reach (destination). pe --- to ripen, grow to maturity. te --- to understand

خوى كيران girán (gr-): xoy pe řa --- to hold o.s. back, restrain o.s.

داكير ساندن girsandín (girsen-): da --- to light, ignite

كير سانەوە girsanəwə́ (girse-) to halt, stop (doing s.th.)

كير وكرفت girugírift difficulty

كيتى gití = gɪtí world, universe

كيزه gizə́ simmering (noise) (onom.)

كت وكو gïftugó conversation, speech, talk

كلان gïlán (gle-) to fall, topple off

كلەى gïləí complaint; (mild) censure

كلەزەردە gïləzərdə́ Gilazarda (village in Sul. Liwa)

64

گل   gі̄l   earth; soil

گر   gïr   flame

گران   gïrán   heavy; expensive; difficult, hard.
--- k. to make heavier

گرد   gïrd   hill

گرنگ   gïrі́ŋ   important

گرتن   gïrtі́n¹ (gr-) to catch; to capture; to hold (capacity). čǝ́nd kǝs ʔǝgre? how many people does it hold? to hold (a meeting). bïgrǝ one might say, it might be said. xoy --- to be secure (by accumulating money, power, etc.), to control o.s. ké ma bu bǝr pekǝnі́n bïtwane xoy bigre? who was there who could restrain his laughter? xoy da --- to hide, conceal o.s. dǝ́st --- bǝ...ǝwǝ to be careful with, be frugal with, not to waste. hǝl --- to lift up; to carry; to take away; to keep, defer (an opinion). řa --- to hire (mercenaries, etc.). wǝr --- to take; to accept, admit s.o.; to win. yǝk --- to become one, unite; to agree with each other, be of the same opinion. wулatǝyǝ̀k gïrtuǝkán the U.S.A. ---ǝ dǝst to take in hand, receive; to assume (charge of)

گرتن   gïrtі́n² capturing; arrest; catching; holding (n.)

گرتهوه   gïrtnǝwé (gïr-ǝwǝ) to cover

گروگک   gïrugі́v sudden movement of any thing; usually subsides soon without achieving any result

گریان   gïryán¹ (gri-) to cry, weep

گریان   gïryán² weeping, crying (n.)

گرژ   gі́rž sullen; morose (face). nawčǝwan-y gïrž k. to frown

گرر   gі́ř flame, blaze

كشت	gĭšt all, all of; the public, people
كشتی	gĭští public; general, all
گڤ	gĭv onom. of sudden movement, e.g. flame, stones, etc.
چون به گژا	gĭž: čún bə ---...da to attack, assault
گیتی	gɪtí, gití world; universe
كوگرد	gogĭ́rd sulpher
گـول	gól goal. --- k. (lə) to score a goal (oñ)
گـولا له	golạlé red anemones
گِـوم	gom pond; lagoon; lake
گومه ره ش	gomərέš Gomeresh (a village near Derbendi Khan dam)
گومرگ	gomérg Gomerg (m.p.n.)
هاتنه گوری	gór: hatnə ---e to come up, come into existence; to come to the forefront
گورانی	goraní song, singing (n.). --- wutín (ḻe-) to sing songs, sing
گوره وی	gorəwí socks, stockings
گـورین	gorín¹ (gor-) to change
گورین	gorín² change; transformation
گورینه ر	gorinér change-producing
گـورر	goř grave, tomb
گورران	gořán (·goře-) to change (intrans.)
گورستان	gořstán graveyard, cemetery
گوشه	gošέ nook, corner, side
گوشت	góšt meat
گـویژه	goyžέ, šax-i --- Mt. Goyzha (a mountain

N.E. of Sul.)

کر   gr-: see gĭr-

هه‌ل گولوفان   gulofán (gulofe-): he̱l --- to rub

گولپ   gúl̶up Gulup (a village in Sul. Liwa)

گومان   gumán doubt. ---i tya nífyə there is no doubt about it. ---ĭm nɪyə I have no doubt. bé --- without doubt, doubtless

گوزه‌ران   guzərán living conditions; means of living, subsistence

گول   gʊl leper

گولله   gʊllé bullet

گولله توپ   gʊllə tóp cannon ball

گول   gúl̶ rose; flower

گولاله سوره   gʊlaləsuré scarlet poppy

گول په‌رست   gùl̶pəríst flower-lover

گونجانن   gʊnjanín (gʊnjan-) (foll. by subjunct.) to chime in with, to suit; to be fitting, appropriate, proper

گورگ   gʊrg wolf. --- əbór Gray Wolf (epithet of a fierce warrior)

گورج   gʊrj quickly, right away

به گورجی   gʊrjí: bə --- quickly, hastily

به گورج وگولی   bə gùrjugol̶í quickly, speedily

له گور   gúř: lə --- abruptly

گوتن   gʊtín dial. var. of wʊtín to say

گوایا   gwáya (conj. introducing subordinate clauses in statements) is it possible...; you mean to say...

گوی   gwe¹ ear. ---y lə...b. to hear. ---m lə mosiqà-i ʕəskərífyə I hear military

music. ---t le bu? did you hear that?
---y dánə to listen to, pay attention
to, heed. ---m nédayə qsə-i kəs I
heeded no one. gwe nádate he doesn't
care, it doesn't bother him. --- g̣ to
listen. -᷄- bĭgrə listen! --- kə̌ř k.
to turn a deaf ear to, ignore. pĭšt ---
xĭstĭn (xə-), xĭstĭn pĭšt --- to be indifferent to, disregard, turn one's back
on

گـوی   gwéᵉ shore; bank; brink; edge

کویچـم   gwečə̃m bank of a small river

گـوی‌دان   gwedán listening(n.)

کوی‌کر   gwegír listener

گـویلا ك   gwelák fəce

به‌گویـه‌ی   gweré: bə ---i according to

کویزه‌ر   gwezér carrots

کیا   gyá grass. s̱əwzə -᷄- green grass

کیان   gyán soul; life. In direct address:
dear! dára gyan Dara, dear! Exclam.:
bravo!

کیانـدار   gyandár living creature

کیان‌له‌به‌ر   gyanləbér a living thing, animate object

غ Υ

فـه‌لـه‌ت   ɣəlét mistake, error

غـیری   ɣéyri except. --- zanyarí nəbet except
education

غـه‌ش   ɣə̌š cheating, deception. be ---əwə in
all honesty

غـه‌زنه‌دار   ɣəznədár treasurer, keeper of the treas-
ury

ه   h

هـــا há (interj.) well, now! there! there
you are!

هـانـدان han d. to instigate; to tempt

هـانـدان handán instigation

هـاره‌ی پیکه‌نین harə-i pekənín an outburst of laughter

هاتن hatín (ye-[dial. var.=de-], does not take
aspect prefix: yem 'I come'; subjunct. stem:
be-: bem 'that I come'; impert. stem: wə́řə
'come!') to come. hatmə jəwáb I answered.
bəsər...(da)--to befall, happen to. čí
bəsər hat? what happened to him? da ---
to come about, take place; to set in, fall
(darkness). həl --- to run away, flee,
escape. lə...--- to befall, happen to;
to suit, become, be becoming to s.o.
hər lə xót ye it only suits you. pek
--- to be formed; to come about. --- bə
dwa...da to come after, come to get s.o.
hat bə dwa kuřəkəyda she came after her
son. --- bəsər to befall, happen to.
hatnə to come to. (lə) hatnə də́re to
come out (of), emerge (from). řoh lə
jegəyek-i sə́xtayə wənáyetə də̀re the soul
is in an inaccessible place and so never
emerges (an expression of great emotional
upheaval - joy, anger, pain, etc.). ---ə
dí to come into existence; to be realized. ---ə gó̀re to come into existence,
come up, arise. ---ə náw...əwə to come
into, enter. ---ə sə́r to come to,
arrive at. ---ə xwarəwə to come down,
descend, alight.

هاتن و چوون hatínučún to come and go; to move to
and fro

هاتنه‌وه hatnəwə́ (ye-; subjunct. be-; imperative:
wə́řəwə) to come back. return. cf.
hatín. lə...--- to come out of

هاوار hawár screaming, wailing; appeal. ʔə́y
---! bravo! hə́y --- help! --- k. to
cry out (in pain), great outcry; wailing (n.)

هاوبه‌ش   hawbéš partner. ---i...b. to take part, participate in s.th.

هاوبه‌شی کردن له...دا   hawbəší k. lə...da to participate in

هاوین   hawín summer

هاوشتن   hawĭštĭn (haw-) to throw

هاوکاری کردن   hawkarí k. to coach; to advise on

هاوولاتی   hawḻatí fellow countryman

هاوری   hawřé companion, friend

هاوسنور   hawsĭnúr a common border with

هاوتا   hawtá equal, par. ləgəḻ...da --- k. to compare s.th. with...

هاییه‌خت   haybéxt: bitaqə-i --- lottery ticket

هیجگار   hejgár permanent; in particular, particularly; Preceding the adj. it modifies: extremely, very

هیجگاری   hejgarí completely, totally; permanently

هیلکه   helké egg(s)

هیمن کردنه‌وه   hemĭn k.əwə to slow down (trans.)

هین   hén = hín the one of; belonging to, ...'s. lə henəkè-i xóy gəle zortĭrə it is much more than his own

هینان   henán (hen-; subjunct., imperat. stem: ben-) to bring. da --- to comb. dər --- to take out, remove (from: lə) to pull out; to root out; to extract; to produce; to refine. həl --- to bring into being, produce s.th. bə kar --- to put into use; to use, utilize. pek --- to bring together, unite; to put together, arrange; to form; to create; to bring about, make materialize. ---ə dí to implement, put into effect. ---ə sér... to bring s.th. over...

70

هێنانەوە   henanǝwǝ́ (hen-) to bring s.th. back, return s.th. --- sǝr xóy to bring s.o.
back to consciousness

هێرش   herǐ̆š attack; onslaught; army (for attack);
any large number of people. ٦-- bǐ̈rdnǝ
sǝr (bǝ-) to launch an army against,
attack, storm. --- henàn bo sǝ́r to
launch an attack on

هێرشهێنەر   herǐ̆šhenǝ́r attacker, attacking (adj.)

هێشتا   héšta yet; still

هێشتن   heštǐ̆n (heḻ-, yeḻ-) (foll. by subjunct.)
to permit, allow, let (s.o. do s.th.);
Neg.: to wipe out s.o.

هـــێـــز   hez power, strength, force. bǝ ---
strong, powerful. --- lǝ... bǐ̈rrán (pass.
of bǐ̈rin) to be completely sapped of
strength. lǝbǝr pekǝnín ---yan lǝ
bǐ̈rráwǝ they are weak from laughter

هەبوون   hǝbún (hǝ- + pron. suff. + bún: pres.
hémǝ, hétǝ, héyeti; hémanǝ, hétanǝ,
héyanǝ; past. hǝmbu, etc.) to have.
pǐ̈rsyárekǐ̈m heyǝ I have a question.
boy --- kǝ (foll. by subjunct.) to have
the power, right, prerogative to do s.th.
bóm heyǝ kǝ bínermǝwǝ I have the right
to send him back. héyǝ (neg. níyǝ) there
is, there are. štek-i wà níyǝ there is
no such thing. ʔímřo čí heyǝ what's
going on today? ʔǝbe ʔǝdǝb-i kurdi
hébet yan nábet necessarily, either
Kurdish literature exists or it does
not exist. hébew nèbe perhaps. ---
bǝxti krawǝtǝwǝ perhaps he has had a
stroke of luck

هەچ   hǝč many

هەل   hǝl opportunity

هەلاتن   hǝḻatín = hǝḻ hatín to run away, flee;
escape

هەلبەست   hǝḻbə́st verse, poetry

هەلبژارد ن	həlbī́žardī́n election
هەلبژ یرراو	həlbī́žeřáw selected; select (adj.)
هەلچوو	hə̰lčú shooting up. balá --- tall
هەله	hə̰lé error, mistake. xoy --- k. to deceive o.s.
هەلەداوان	hələdawán: bə --- quickly, hurriedly, arŭnning
هەلگەرراو	həlgəřáw (part. of həl gəřán) changed, turned, transformed. zərd --- yellowish; pale
هەلم	hélĭm steam, vapor
هەلكەندراو	həlkəndráw engraved, inscribed
بە هەلمەت	həlmét: bə --- ready to attack; aggressive
هەلمەتی	həlmətí vigor in grappling; fierceness
هەلو	hə̰ló eagle; vulture
بە هەلپە	hə̰lpé: bə --- gallant; heroic
هەلپەرین	həlpəřín dancing; to dance
هەلپەرکی	hə̰lpəřké dance, dancing; folk dancing
هەمان	həmán the same
هەمه	həmé (with foll. n.) of all; having all, omni-, multi-. həmərəŋé multicolored. həmèjoré of all varieties
هەمیشه	həmišé always
هەمیشەیی	həmišəí sustained, continuous
هەمو	həmú Foll. by noun or pron. suff.: all, all of. həmú zĭstan all winter (long). həmítan all of you. ʔərz ---y sə́wzbu the land wall all green. Foll. by n. plus -ek: each, every. həmú zĭstanek every winter. --- štek everything. lə --- layek on all sides. --- jorəkĭštukalek tya ʔəkre every kind of crop is cultivated there.

72

هه مزه	həmzə́ the letter ' (glottal stop)
هه ن	hə́n they exist, are. see bún
هه نار	hənár pomegranates
هه ناسه	hənasə́ breath
هه ناسه ساردی	hənasəsardí lamentation, regret, dis-appointment
هه ناو	hənáw bosom; inner part
هه نديك	hənd: hə́ndek, hə́nde (lə) some, several. --- jar several times
هه نسك	həni̇́sk sobbing, choking (n.)
هه نجير	hənjír figs
هه نگاو	həŋáw step, stride. --- nán (ne-) to take a step
هه ر	hə́r only, alone, just. --- ʔəwánïn kə they are the only ones who... --- lə́mčayxanèda in just this teahouse alone. --- ʔəbé one can only... --- pére just the day before yesterday. ba --- qsə nə́kəm I'd better not say anything! even; already; the very. --- lə kat-i fərmandarì ʔəwábu it was thus also during his rule. --- ʔə́wiš he is the very one... all. bə --- čwar la-i xóma all around me, on all four sides, certainly, surely. ʔəginá hər sə́ri̇m ʔəday otherwise I would certainly have visited you. Foll. by n. plus -ek: each, every; any. --- yékek each one. --- bəšdárek any subscriber. Foll. by n. plus -é: every, any. --- kəsé everybody; anybody. --- řožé every day. --- kə (foll. by subjunct.) as soon as. see also compounds, e.g., hərdú, hərčóne, hərwéku, etc.
هه را	hərá trouble, commotion; great noises
هه راج کردن	həraj k. to auction off
هه راو هوریا	həràwhoryá yelling and shouting; troubles; confusion

73

هه ر چه ند hərčə́nd, hərčə́ndə although, even though; no matter how much; whenever. ---...bélam although... still...

هه ر چی hərčí whatever; every, everyone

هه ر چو نيك hərčónek be[t], ---bu at any rate, in any case

هه رد وو hérdu both. --- kəs both people. hérduk both of. hérdukman both of us. ---yan both of them

هه ره س hərə́s avalanche, onslaught, sudden fall (of rocks, etc.). --- henán (hen-) to collapse, tumble down

هه رگز hərgíz (with neg.) never. --- lə bir náx̌nəwə (I) will never forget them. in no way, not at all. --- níyə it does not exist at all

هه ركه س hérkəs anybody

هه ر می hərmé pears

هه ررا كرد ن hərra k. = řa k. to run, run away

هه روا hérwa in the same way, likewise

هه روه ها hérwəha similarly, likewise

هه روه ك hərwə́k in a similar manner; just as

هه روه كو hərwəkú at the same time

هه ريه كه héryəkè each one

هه رزان hərzán cheap; inexpensive

هه رزه كار hərzəkár young, quite young

هه ره شه həřəšə́ threat; warning

هه ست həst feeling, sentiment. --- bə...k. to sense, be aware of s.th. --- k. bə... to feel, sense s.th.

هه ستان = هه لستان həstán (həl-s-) = həl stán to arise

74

هه شت	héšt	eight
هه شتا	həštá	eighty
هه شتهم	həštém	eighth
هه تا	hətá, tá, hətáku	until, up to; even. Foll. by subjunct.: in order that
هه تاهات	hətàhát	gradually
هه تاکو	hətáku = hətá	until
هه تاو	hətáw	sun
هه تاوکه وتن	hətawkəwtín	sunrise
هه تاههتی	hətayí: həta ---	for ever, from now till eternity; (with neg.) never
هه تیو	hətíw	orphan. Used vocatively. hétiw! to show displeasure
هتد	hétɪd	etc.
هه وا	həwá¹	air, breeze, wind
هه وا	həwá²	a little bit
هه وایی	həwaí	of the air
هه وال	həwál	news tidings. --- wáy gəyand we have received word of...
هه وه س	həwés	merriment
هه ور	həwír	cloud(s)
هه ول	héwl	endeavor. --- dán (kə foll. by subjunct.) to try (to do s.th.)
هه ولیر	həwlér	Arbil
هه ولیری	həwlerí	Arbilite
هه ولوته ته لا	həwlutəqəlá	great endeavor
هه ورامان	həwramán	Hawraman; Awraman (mountain range in N.E.Iraq and N.W.Iran)

75

هه ورامی	həwramí of or pertaining to Hawraman
هه وه ل	həwwél first. lə -́-əwə from the first; at the outset. cf. ʔəwwél
هه ی	həy (ejaculation sometimes used in responses to questions)
هه یه	héyə there is, there are. see həbún
هه ینی	həyní Friday
هه زار	həzár thousand. bíst --- kə̀s ʔəgre it holds 20,000 people. həzarán, həzarəhá thousands (n.)
هه ژار	həžár poor
هه ژاری	həžarí poverty
هه ژده	həždé eighteen
هسی	hi (the one) of, belonging to. --- ʔəhméd bu it was Ahmed's. --- mínə it is mine. --- həmí gə̀l-i kurdə it belongs to all Kurdish people
هیـلاك	hilák tired, exhausted. hilákbuyn we got tired
هـیوا	hiwá hope, aspiration. ---y bə...b. kə (foll. by subjunct.) to rely, depend on... to (do s.th.). --- wáyə the hope is, it is hoped that... ---i žɩyán lə... k. to expect...to live
هیوادار	hiwadár hopeful
هـجری	hïjrí A.H., in the year from the Hegira; abbreviated ـه
هچ	hɩč any, anything. ---i tïr? anything else? With neg.: no, nothing. ---yan none of them. ---nébe (nébwayə) at least. bə --- jórek at all.
هچوپچ	hɩčupúč meaningless; worthless
هو	ho cause, reason. ---i sərəkí the main reason. bə ---i because of. bə ---i...əwə by means of. b. bə ---i... to result in, cause s.th.

ح   ẖ 2

حافيز   ẖafíz   protector.   xwa ---   goodbye

حاجى   ẖají   pilgrim (who has made the pilgrimage to Mecca),   <u>hajji   salíh</u>   Hajji Salih

حاكـم   ẖakím   governor

حـال   ẖál   (pl. ẖalán)   condition, state

حاميه   ẖamıyə́   barracks, garrison

حاسه   ẖasə́   (pl. ẖəwás)   sense.   ---i mušterə́k common sense.   ---i šəšə́m   the sixth sense

حازر   ẖazír   present, ready

حـب   ẖəb   pills.   ---i žanəsə́r   headache pills

حـفتا   ẖəftá   seventy

حـفته ، هـفته   ẖəftə́   week

حـلال   ẖəlál   legitimate; legitimately earned. mal-i --- lə də́stit nə́čet   you will not lose money honestly earned

حـلـوا   ẖəlwá   halwa (local candies made of manna and sugar)

حـمال   ẖəmál   porter

حـمام   ẖəmám   bath; (public) bathhouse

حـمه   ẖəmə́   (dim. of mĭẖəmmed)   Muhammad

حمله   ẖəmlə́   attack; campaign

حـمو   ẖəmú   see ẖəmú   all

حـپاندن   ẖəpandín   (ẖəpεn-)   to bark

حـپه   ẖəpə́   barking (n.)

حـق ، هـق   ẖəq   (pl. ẖquq)   right (n.), justice

حـراره   ẖərarə́   temperature.   dərəjə-i --- temperature

77

حەرەكات	ḫərəkát movement, motion
حەرەم	ḫərém family part of the house (formerly, the houses of the rich were divided into diwaxán, for guests, and ḫərém, where the family itself lived.)
حەریر ، هەریر	ḫərír Harir (area near Rawandúz noted for its plains)
حەسانەوە	ḫəsanəwé[1] (ḫəse-) to rest, repose
حەسانەوە	ḫəsanəwé[2] comfort, relaxation, rest
حەسەن	ḫəsén Hassan
حەڤدە	ḫəvdé, ḫəvvé seventeen
حەوانەوە	ḫəwanəwé (ḫəwe-) to live in comfort or luxury (after hard work)
حەواس	ḫəwás pl. of ḫasé sense
حەوشە	ḫəwšé courtyard (of a house, completely enclosed)
حەوت	ḫəwt seven
حەوز	ḫəwz pool; pond
حەیف	ḫéyf wrong, injustice, harm. --- níyə ʔemə lə xošída beyn there is no harm in our enjoying ourselves
حیوان	ḫəywán (ḫəywanát) animal
حەز لی كردن	ḫəz lə...k. to like; to love. ḫézi le ʔəkəm I like it. --- ʔəkəm bírôm I would like to go
حەزرەت	ḫəzrét hezret (title of respect used before names of prophets) ---i sʊləymán the prophet Solomon
حیزباب	ḫizbáb fat father (pejorative)
حكومەت	ḫïkumét government. ---i ʕiráq the government of Iraq
حلمی	ḫïlmí Hilmi (m.p.n.)

78

حسين   h̲ïsén   Hussain

حكمت   h̲ıkmét   Hikmet (m.p.n.)

حيزب   h̲ízb   party. ---i ʔəhrár   the Liberal Party. ---i dimuqratï   the Democratic Party. ---i jəmhurí   the Republican Party

حمهد   h̲məd = ʔəh̲méd   Ahmad

حقوق   h̲quq (pl. of h̲əq)   rights (legal)

حوكم   h̲úkum   power, authority; rule, government

حوزهيران   h̲uzəyrán   June

ى   i   (See also ʔi)

-iš (after vowel -š) also, too. Often points out an opposing party: for (his) part; while... ʔəméš bašə this one also is good. ʔeméš həyn we too exist. náxoməwəw náškešïm I don't drink, nor do I smoke. léwlašəwə on the other side also. xóši wut he himself also said... ʔəw...wəʔeméš he...while we...

ج   j

جا   já   then, therefore, hence; well then. --- kə now that... --- wéř̌ə just come and...

جاده   jaddé   street. ---i ř̌ast straight streets

جام   jam   bowl; glass, pane of glass

جامعه   jamiʕé   university

جان   jan   soul

جاندرمه   jandïrmé   gendarme; policeman

79

جانه وه ر   janəwér   monster

جانتا   jantá   suitcase; wallet; portfolio

جـــار   jar   time (of occurrence). --- bə ---
occasionally, at times. həmí --- always.
dú --- twice. bo ---i duwém for the
second time. bə yék --- at the same time.
ʔəmə yekém jaryeti ʔəče this is her first
time to go... járe meantime, first (let's),
just. járe tozek dánišin ʔɪnja pékəwə
ʔəcinə ʔəwe let't just sit down for a bit
then we'll go there together. bə járe all
at once; completely, thoroughly. həmíy bə
járe all at once. -´-ek-i tĭr another
time; the next time. jarán formerly. ---i
jarán former times, days gone by. jarjár
from time to time

جاره كى   jarəkí   temporary; passing; transient

جار جار   jarjár   every now and then, from time to
time. cf. jar

جار و بار   jarubár   occasionally

جاش   jaš   foal of the ass

جـــى   je   place, position. ʔéw---yə xóšə kə
dĭḻ tya xóšbe any place is nice when
one is happy there. ---i dĭlgiríyə kə...
it is a matter of regret that... be ---
unsuitable. bə --- suitable. --- bə
--- suitable, proper; in order. bə ---
henán to complete, bring to completion;
to follow (a practice), adhere to (a rule).
...bə --- heštĭn (hel-, yel-) to leave,
leave behind. --- bə̄ --- k̄. to put into
effect; to grant; to perform,execute.
bə --- mán (men-) to be left behind, be
overlooked

جى به جى كردن   jebəjekĭrdĭn   execution, performance (of
a task); disposing (n.)

جێگا   jegá   place, position. ---i kobunəwəké
the meeting place. ---y lə mežú his
place in history. --- bo... k. to prepare a place for...

جيماو   jemáw legacy, heritage

جه غفه ری   jəʕfərí Jaʕfari, follower of Jaʕfar, Shiite

جه هه نه م   jəhənnám hell

جــلاله ت   jəlalát majesty

جه ماعه ت   jəmaʕát group

جه ماهير   jəmahír people, the masses; the public

جه مال   jəmál Jamal (m.p.n.)

جه مهوریه ت   jəmhuriyát republic

جه نگ   jáŋ war; fight; fighting (n.)

جه نگی   jəŋí pertaining to fighting; fighter

جه رگ   jərg heart, liver, etc. (fig., seat of emotions). dáxi bə -́-ĭm (bo...) alas (for...)!

جه رگه   jərgá innermost part (of a person). lə náw -́-i...da in the innermost part of, in the bowels of

جه ریده   jəridá newspaper

جه ریده چی   jəridəčí journalist

جه ریمه   jərimá crime

جه واب   jəwáb answer. --- d.əwá to answer. ʔəməwe bzánĭm čónĭm jəwáb ʔədatəwə I want to see how he will answer me

جه واهــیری   jəwahirí Jawahiri (m.p.n.)

جه وال   jəwá‌l saddlebag

جه وهه ر   jəwhár essence. bə --- keen; of powerful personality

جيش   jəyš army

جه زا   jəzá a fine. --- lə...sandĭn to fine s.o. čónĭm le səŋrá how much was I fined?

jəzaʔír

جزائر	jəzaʔír Algeria; Algiers
جەزرەبه دان	jəzrəbə lə...d. to do harm to, injure s.o.
جەژن	jéžĭn feast, festival, anniversary, holiday. ---i nəwróz New Year's holiday. ---i čwardə-i təmmíz the July 14th Festival
جیهــان	jihán world
جبەخانه	jĭbəxané ammunition
جگەلــه	jĭgəl(l)ə...(tĭr) except, except for. --- sərbəxoí- řastəqiné, sərbəstí- tĭri náwe ...does not want any freedom except genuine independence. With neg.: only. jĭgəlləwə in addition to that, besides which. bé jĭgəlləwə except for; furthermore. jĭgəlləwə-i kə except that (conj.); in addition to which
جگەر	jĭgér liver; insides (of a person)
جگەره	jĭgəré cigarette. --- kešán (keš-) to smoke (cigarettes)
جگەرگوشه	jĭgərgošé of one's own blood; one's own kin; a very dear person
جگەرسوتاو	jĭgərsutáw person heavily afflicted with misfortune (usually death of a close relative)
جــل	jĭl clothes. --- ləbər k. to put on clothes; to get dressed
جل وبەرگ	jĭlubérg clothes, apparel
جلــفا	jĭlfá slang
جمهوریەت	jĭmhuriyét = jəmhuriyét republic
جناب	jĭnab: jĭnábtan you (sg.: honorific usage). jnàbtan nàwtan číyə what is your name?
جنیو	jĭnéw abuse, insult, cursing. --- d. bə to curse at s.o. jĭnéwi pe dam he cursed at me

جنيودان	jïnewdán cursing; revilement, abusive language
جنوب	jïnúb south
جنوبى	jïnubí southern, south (adj.)
جزيره	jïziré island
جن	jn- see jïn-
جو	jó barley
جولا	jolá weaver
جور	jór kind, sort, type. bém---ə in this way. bə híč ---ek in no way. bémjorə-karəsatanè in this kind of disaster. bə ---ek-i wá (wəhá) (kə) (foll. by subjunct.) in such a way that...
جوش	još boiling, ferment. --- d. to boil. hatnə -́- to be ablaze, on fire; to be dancing with excitement
جوشوخروش	jošuxróš movement, activity
جوييار	joybár small river, stream
جوغرافـيا	juɣrafɪyá geography
جوغرافيازان	juɣrafɪyazán geographer
جو	ju, juləké Jew
جـودا	judá different
جوجەلە	jujəlé chick
جولەكە	juləké Jew
جولان	juḻán (juḻe-) to move; to jerk
جولانەوه	juḻanəwé¹ (juḻe-) to move s.th.; to act
جولانەوه	juḻanəwé² movement; activity; exercises (mĩl.); event. -́-yek ʔəxatə ʔémnawčəyè it brings activity to this region
جـرون	jun (ju-) to chew (gum, etc.)

83

جـــووت	jut pair, couple. --- b. ləgəl...da to form a pair with; to be on a par with, be the same as
جــووته	juté couples; twins
جومعه	jumʕé Friday
جوملـه	jumlé sentence
جوتیار	jʊtyár peasant; farmer
جـــواب	jwab = jəwáb answer. hatmə -́- I answered
جـــوان	jwan¹ beautiful. --- k. to beautify s.th. jwantĭrĭm kĭrd I made it even more beautiful
جــوان	jwan² Jwan (f.p.n.)
جـواندهرگ	jwanəmérg a person who dies before his time, one who dies young. -́--bĭm qĭsə nákəm may I die young if I speak!
جـوانــی	jwaní beauty
جـوانپەرستی	jwanpərĭstí love of beauty
جـوی	jwé different. --- b. ləgəl to be different from. ʔéwpezaninè -́--yə ləgəl həwas-i xəmsé that (kind of) knowing is different from the five senses
جــیا	jya separate; different
لـه جیاتـی	jyatí: lə --- instead of, in place of; on behalf of. lə --- ʔəwə-i (foll. by subjunct.) instead of (conj.). wə lə --- ʔəwə-i bĭbe bə... and instead of its becoming...
جیاواز	jyawáz different
جیاوازی	jyawazí difference. (lə niwán: between). bə ---i-...əwə regardless of...

ك   k

كـا   ka   straw

كابا   kabá   Kaba

كابينه   kabiné   cabinet

كابرا   kabrá   person, man; fellow

كافــر   kafír   infidel, blasphemer, atheist

كاغذ   kaɣéz   paper, sheet of paper; letter,
           epistle

كاهــو   kahú   lettuce

كاك   kak   elder brother.   káka (title of res-
           pect used in direct address to an elder
           brother or any older male)

كاكه ناس kakənás   shovel

كاكی به كاكی   kakí: --- bə ---   vast, enormous (plain)

كالیار   kalyár   a kind of cucumber

كال   kal̲   light (in color); raw (food)

كالـك   kal̲ék   melon

كم   kám   which?   -́- pyaw   which man?   ---yan
           řasttïrekə   which of them is most correct?
           ---...-ə   which? (specific)   --- wušəyə
           which (particular) word?   kamané   which ones?
           híč ---ekman (+ neg.)   no one of us

كامه ران kamərán   prosperous

كامه رانی kaməraní   happiness; prosperity

كامیرون   kamirón   Cameroun

كـان   kan   mine, quarry

كانیك   kanék   metal

كانیسكان kaneskán   Kanieskan (a quarter in Sul.)

85

كانــى   kaní¹ spring (water). lə --- dĭlyəwə from the bottom of his heart

كانــى   kaní² mine (n.) (of ore)

كانــون   kanún: ---i duwém, ---i saní January. ---i ʔəwwél, ---i yəkém December

كانگ   kaŋgé source

كـــار   kar word; deed; function; action, course of action; task, errand; prodecure; incident. ʔém---ə nákat it does not perform this task. ---i gér consequential, significant; grave, serious. be --- idle; unemployed; bachelor. bə --- active, lively; industrious. bə --- bĭrdĭn (bə-) to use, employ. bə --- henán to use, utilize, employ. --- həyə bo sér... has effect on... ---ek-i gəwréy həyə bo sər... it has a great effect on... ---k. to use up, consume. ---ek-i wa k. (foll. by subjunct.) to act in such a way as to, make it possible for... ---ek-i wáy kĭrd gəl-i filipín baš bĭzane he gave the Philippine people to understand clearly that... --- k.ə sér to have an effect on, affect, influence. kəwtnə -́- to begin to function, start operating. xĭstnə -́- (xə-) to put s.th. to work; to put s.th. into operation. cf. karé

كاربـدەست   kàrbədést manager, director; influential person; authorities; government official(s)

كاريز   karéz spring (water). cf. kaní

كاره   karé workings; behavior. be --- lazy. čĭkaréyə? what work does he do?

كارەبا   karəbá electricity

كارەسات   karəsát catastrophe, calamity; important events

كارگ   kargé factory

كارى كردن   kari k. to make worse; to cause (a wound) to fester

كاركەر   karkér   workman

كارتامه   kartamé   enterprise, project

كاروبار   karubár   functions, duties, work; the duties of office; events; situation, condition. ---i jihán   the world situation

كاروكاسپ كردن   karukàsp k.   to work, get work done

كاروانسەرا   karwansərá   caravanserai

كارخانه   karxané   factory

كارزار   karzár   combat, battle

كارژوله   karžolé   kid, young goat or sheep

كاسه   kasé   bowl. ---i pĭř ?ašt-i mále   a full bowl and peace at home (prov.)

كات   kát   time, period. ?éw---ə̀   at such a time; in such a case. lə ---i xóyda   in its time; originally. lə zutrìn -´-da   as quickly as possible. lə ---i   at the time of; upon; during. lə -´-ekda   at the time that, while. --- bə bər...əwə mán (men-)   there remains time for... -´-ekĭm zanì   before I realized it, all of a sudden

كاتب   katĭb   secretary. ---i nahyé   secretary of a nahiya

كاوان   kawán   barn

كاوه   kawé   Kawa (name of a Kurdish hero)

كايه   kayé   scene of action. hatĭnə -´-   to come on the scene, appear. henanə -´- to bring on stage; to focus attention on

كاژ   kaž   cover

كاژوله   kažəlé   skull

كسى   ké   who?

كيل   kel   tombstone

كيلان   kelán   scabbard, sheath.   ---i xənjér sheath of a dagger

كيلا ن   kel̲án (⁻kel̲-)   to plough

كيشان   kešán (keš-)   to pull, draw; to weigh. xóm keša   I weighed myself.   jigəré --- to smoke (cigarettes).   se mán̩ənəmkešawə I haven't smoked for three months.   həl ---   to heave out, emit; to eradicate. řa ---   to stretch, draw.

كيشه   kešé   difficulty, complication, thorny problem

كيشەر   kešér   drawing, attracting (adj.)

كـيو   kéw   mountain (usually high and rugged)

كــ   kə¹   who, which (rel.); at the time that, when (rel.); if, when.   ʔəwə-i kə zirékə sér ʔəkəwe   the one who is clever will succeed.   kə gəyštnə bəɣá   when you arrive in Baghdad.   ---...čon   how (adv.). --- ta   as long as.   cf. kəčí but; kəwá that (conj.)

كــ   kə²: -i ---   more, else.   həmí nətəwəkàn-i ké   all the other nations.   salek-i ké one more year.   čə̆ŋ št-i ké ⁻a⁻ few more items.   mĭn hɪč-i kém náwe   I don't want anything else.

كەباب   kəbáb   kabob

كەبابچى   kəbabčí   kabob maker

كە چ كردن   kəč k.   to incline

كە چى   kəčí   whereas, but, and yet, but on the other hand.   mu-i sérĭt spí buwə kəčí mu-i říšĭt hešta řéšə   the hair on your head is white whereas your beard is still black

كەف   kəf   foam.   --- čərandín (čəren-)   to froth at the mouth

كەفتەكار   kəftəkár   sick; decrepit

كەلاوە   kəlawé   remains of a ruined house

كه‌لـيـل   kəlíl   key

كه‌للـه   kəllə́   skull; head

كه‌لان   kəlán: tekəláw   mixed

كـلاش   kəláš   knitted foot-wear

كه‌لـدانى   kəldaní   Chaldean

كه‌له‌شر   kələšér   rooster

كه‌لك   kəlk   use, benefit, advantage. be -́́-
useless. bə -́́- useful, beneficial.
šītek-i zór bə kəlke it is a very useful
thing. --- b. tō have effect. Neg.: to
be of no avail. --- pewə b. to be of
benefit to s.o.

كه‌لكبه‌خش   kəlkbə́xš   advantageous

كـم   kəm   few, little (in quantity). -́́-ek
a few, some. bə la-i ---əwə at least.
číman kəmtīrə léwgəlanə̀ what are we
more lacking in than those countries?
--- k.əwə́ to decrease, lessen; to make
little of, deprecate

كه‌م ده‌ست   kəmdə́st   needy

كه‌مه‌نچه   kəmənčə́   violin

كه‌مه‌ر   kəmə́r   waist

كه‌مه‌ربه‌ند   kəmərbə́nd   girdle; sash

كه‌مه‌ره   kəmərə́   arch

كه‌م گوشت   kəmgóšt   lean, slim

كه‌م هـيز   kəmhéz   weak

كه‌مى   kəmí   paucity

كه‌موله   kəmolə́   jug; bowl

كه‌هره‌نگ   kəmřəŋ   light (color)

كه‌مته‌رخه‌م   kəmtərxə́m   indifferent; indifference

89

kəmukuří

كه م وكوردى	kəmɪkuří shortcomings, faults, defects
كه م وزور	kə̀muzór more or less, in the least
كه نسار	kənár brim
كه ند	kənd cliff, chasm
كه ندن	kəndín (kənd-, kən-) to dig. da --- to take off, doff. həḻ --- to carve out; to engrave
كه ندا	kənədá Canada
كه نين	kənín: (bə...) pe --- to laugh (at). péyan pə ʔəkənín they laugh at them. řə́ŋə pey bĭkə́ni perhaps you will laugh at him
كه نيسه	kənisə́ church
كه ر	kər donkey
كه ره	kərə́ butter
كه رهنا	kərəná horn, bugle
كريم	kərím¹ glorious
كريم	kərím² Karim (m.p.n.)
كه ركوك	kərkúk Kirkuk
كه ركوكى	kərkukí Kirkukite
كه رسه ك	kərsə́k clods of earth, loam or clay
كه ر	kəř deaf. gwe lə...--- k. to turn a deaf ear to, ignore
كه س	kəs person. -́-ek lə ʔemə́ any one of us. lə dérəwə --- nábini you won't see anybody out of doors. kəsán (pl.) people; everybody. hə́r---, hə́r---e (foll. by subjunct.) anyone who... híč --- nobody
كه ساس	kəsás pathetic; miserable
كه سوكار	kəsukár people; community; relations, kin

90

كەشف   kəšf discovery. --- k. to discover

كەشتەوان   kəštewán boatman

كەشتى   kəští ship

كەتان   kətán flax, linen

كەو   kəw partridge

كەوا   kəwá that (conj.), a thing that...

كەوان   kəwán a bow

كەوانە   kəwané parenthesis

كەواتە   kəwatá then, in that case

كەوچك   kəwčī́k spoon

كەودان   kəwdán stupid

كەوش   kəwš a kind of shoe

كەوتن   kəwtī́n (kəw-) to fall, fall down, drop (intr.) (-ə: into); to be found, located, situated (-ə, lə: in); to become. kèwtmə ḥəwzəké I fell into the fountain. s̄lemaní šárekə kəwtútə šmal-i šərq-i ʕiraqə Sulaimania is a city found in N.E. Iraq. ʔəkəwīn hər xərikīn... they become completely absorbed in... bə...da --- to be satisfied with... dər --- to appear; to be clear, apparent, evident (boː to s.o.) (lə...əwəː from s.th.); to gain profit. ʔəstərəkán dèr kəwtī́n the stars appeared. bər čáw ʔəkəwīn they become as plain as day, quite apparent. wá dər ʔəkəwe kə... it appears that, apparently. wám bo dər ʔəkəwe it seems to me. həl --- lə... to come forth, emanate from. lə...--- to stop (doing s.th.). peš --- to move forward, advance, progress. žapon zór peš kəwtúwə Japan is very advanced. peš...--- to be more advanced than. peš ʔemé kəwtúwə it is more advanced than we are. ---ə to come to, come upon; to come into; to start (doing s.th.); to begin (to be...). xoší ʔəkəwetə dilməwə pleasure fills my heart. ---ə

91

naw... to meet, join s.o. kəwtmə nawyan I met them, joined them. ---ə xwáre to fall off of, down (from); to roll down

كه وتنه وه   kəwtnəwé (kəw-) to fall again; to spread over. cover s.th.

كــــى ؟   kéy? when?

كه يه ك   kəyék bran

كه يف   kəyf merriment, having a good time

كه زاوه   kəžawé sedan chair

كــغم   kɣm = kiloɣrám kilogram

كيلوغرام   kiloɣrám kilogram abbrev. كغم

كيلومه تر   kilométɪr kilometer

كيميا   kimyá chemistry

كينيا   kinyá Kenya

كيسه   kisé bag, sack

كــچ   kĭč girl; virgin; daughter

كچه زا   kĭčəzá daughter son(s) or daughter(s)

كــفر   kĭfĭr blasphemy. ---i...k. to blaspheme against. ---i dwanzó ʔɪmam ʔəka he blasphemes against the Twelve Imams

كـفن   kĭfn shroud

كــل   kĭl kohl

كليسه   kĭlisé church

كلك   kĭlk tail

به هيچ كلوجيك   kĭlój: bə hfč ---ek in no way, by no means

كلا و   kĭláw head-dress; cap

كلــول   kĭlól miserable; pitiful; humble, servile

كلپه   kĭḻpé   blaze, flame

كـن   kĭ̧n   side.   lə kĭ̧n...əwə   beside.   lə kĭnməwə dá nišə   sit beside me

كـراس   kĭrás   dress; shirt

كرده وه   kĭrdəwé   deed, acts; feats; behavior, conduct. bə --- heroic

كـــردن   kĭrdín (kə-)   to do; to make; to work, manufacture, prepare. čí ʔəkəy   what are you doing? lə bírtə čĭ kĭra   do you recall what happened? mékə to!   don't you do that! ...bə dər k.   to remove s.o. from... šar bə dérĭt ʔəkəm   I'll chase you out of town. da ---   to pour down (: rain). dər ---   to remove, take out; to expel; to promulgate, enact (a law). kə parétbu məla lə mĭzgəwt dér ʔəkəyt   if you have money you can remove a mulla from a mosque (prov.). həḻ ---   to stay, remain; to hoist; to blow (wind, troubles); le ---   to do s.th. with s.th., dispose of s.th. čí le bĭkəm   what shall I do with it?...ləbər ---   to put on, don, wear. jĭl-i páki ləbər kĭrd   he put on some clean clothes. pe ---   to be able to do s.th. about s.th. híčyan pe nékrawə   they have not been able to do anything about it. pe ---   to make s.o. do s.th. ʔišĭt pe ʔəkəm   I'll put you to work. ʔəbé řawəžíškekĭt pe bĭkəm   I must send you on a snipe hunt. pewə --- to trap, ensnare. pəyda ---   to secure, obtain. řa ---   to run away, flee. řo ---ə   to pour s.th. (naw: into); to transfer s.th. from one place to another. řonəkə řó bĭkərə naw ʔémqapə   pour the ghee into this dish. dan řo kĭrdín bo mriškəkán pewístə   it is necessary to give feed to the chickens. te ---   to fill s.th. (as opp. to pĭř k., to fill s.th. up full); ... ---ə...əwə   to put, pour, empty s.th. into... ...---ə, --- bə   to make, turn s.th. into s.th. (lə...əwə: from). ləlayən məhmú kráwə bə kurdí   it was translated into Kurdish by Mahmoud. ...--- bə...da   to throw s.th. at; to grab; to snatch and make off with. xoy

--- bə to thrust o.s. into; to plunge
into. bó xot kïrd bə žer xanu-i řuxáwəwə
why did you plunge into that crumbling
house?

کردنه وه   kïrdnəwé (kə-) to open (door, book, etc.);
to inaugurate (conference, etc.); to
kindle (fire, etc.)

کریکار   kïrekár laborer, worker

کرم   kïrím worms

کرمانجی   kïrmanjí Kurmanji

کروین   kïřín to buy

کرنوش   kïřúš: --- bo...bïrdín to cringe before

کشتوکال   kïštukál agriculture. --- k. to plant,
cultivaŧe

کشتوکالی = کشتوکال   kïštukalí = kïštukál agriculture

کتیب   kïtéb book

کتیب خانه   kïtebxané bookshop

کز   kïz dull, weak (light); inactive; slow
(commerce). čïraké ---ə the lamp is
weak. bazár ---ə business is slow.

کفته   kïfté kifta, a grilled hamburger-like
dish

کلاسیکی   klasikí classical

کلاو   klaw cap

کلاوکوره   klawkuré lark

کسو   ko: ko b.əwé to gather, assemble (intr.).
lə...---b.əwə to gather around s.o. ---
k.əwé to gather, collect s.o., s.th.

کوبونه وه   kobunəwé meeting, assembly; gathering (n.)

کوچ   koč departure. --- k. to depart, leave.
---i dwaì k. to pass away, die

كوليره   koleré loaf of bread

كولين   kolín (kol-) to dig

كولينه‌وه   kolinəwé (kol-): le --- to dig out; to extract; to clarify; to think over, ponder, study carefully

كـول   kól burden, load. --- d. to give up, quit (trying)

كـولان   kolán lane, street

كـومار   komár republic

به‌ كومه‌ك   komék: bə --- in cooperation, collaboration; jointly

كومه‌كى   koməkí collaboration

كومه‌ل   komél group; organization; society. bə --- in groups

كومه‌لا یه‌تى   koməlayətí society; social

كـون   kon old, ancient (things). řəfiq-i --- old friends. hər lə ---əwə even in ancient times. lə zór ---əwə from the most ancient times

كونه‌په‌رست   konəpəríst reactionary

كونغرانس   konfïráns conference

كونگره   koŋgré congress; conference

كـور   kor group (of people); center of activity; festivity

كـوسپ   kosp obstacle; difficulty; impediment

كـوش   kóš lap

تیكوشان   košan (koš-): te --- to struggle, strive

كوشش   košïš great endeavor, effort; struggle

كوشك   košk large building; palace

کوتایی	kotaí end. --- pe hatín = --- bə... henán to bring...to an end, conclude
کوته	koté manacles, shackles; chains
کوتر	kotír dove
کوتره‌حه‌مامی	kotrəhəmamí homing pigeon
کوخت	kox́t hut, cottage
کوزمان	kozĭmán academy (e.g., language academy)
پی کران	pe kran (= passive of kĭrdín) to be possible. čéndyan pe bĭkre as many as possible
کسری	kře rent
کشان	kš́án (kš-) to rush along, go ahead (bo: to)
کولاو	kuḻáw boiled
کوونه‌گورگ	kunəgúrg wolf-hole; a hole in the ground
کونه‌لوت	kunəlút nose
کور	kur hunchback
کوروزی	kuruzé coldness, freezing cold
کوژانه‌وه	kužán...əwə (kuž́én-) to extinguish
کول	kʋl dull (knife, etc.)
کوله	kʋllé locust
کلیه	kʋllıyé college
به کول	kʋḻ: bə --- with an outburst; hearty
کولان	kʋḻán (kʋḻe-) to boil
کولك	kʋḻk chicken ready to lay eggs
کونجی	kʋnjí sesame
کورد	kʋrd Kurd

96

کورده‌واری   kurdəwarí   the Kurdish people

کـــــوردی   kurdí   Kurdish; Kurdish language

کـــوردستان   kurdĭstán, kʋrdʋstán   Kurdistan

کـــــورتی   kurtí   shortness. bə --- in short, in brief

کـــورت و دریژی   kʋrtudrežĭ́   shortness and length

کـــــور   kuř   boy; son. kúřə you, boy! yəzid-i kuř-i mʋʕawıyé Yazid the son of Muʕawiya. ---ané boy-like; bravely, fearlessly

کـــوریتی   kuřetĭ́   boyhood; bravery

کوره کاژاو   kuřəkažáw   Kurakajaw (a high mountain in Iraq)

کـــوره زا   kuřəzá   son's son(s) or daughter(s)

کـــوشتار   kʋštár   slaughter, carnage

کـــوشتن   kʋštĭn (kʋž-)   to kill, murder

کـــوتان   kʋtán (kʋte-)   to strike, hit; to hammer. da --- to drive s.th. in (nails, roots, etc.). bĭnji lə náwmana dá kʋtawə it has become deeply rooted among us. xoy --- to go to; to sneak into (a place) (-ə, bərəw, bo: to)

کـــوتوپڕ   kʋtupĭ́ř   all of a sudden, suddenly

کـــوژانه‌وه   kužanəwé (kʋže-)   to go out, burn out, be extinguished (light, etc.)

کـــــوا   kwa   where is... -´- kuřəkèm where is my son?

کـــوارك   kwarĭ́k   mushroom

کـــوی   kwe   where? what place? bo --- where to? lə --- in what place? where? bə hér ---yekda wherever

کـــویر   kwer   blind

کـــویره‌واری   kwerəwarí   predicament

97

کـــویری   kwerí blindness

کـــویستانـــی   kwestaní northern

ل 1

ل   la side; direction. ʔémlayə ʔəmyešé
this side (of mine) hurts. ʔémlaw ʔéwla
this side and that, both sides. hérdu
layan both sides. lə hér čwar ---i
jihánəwə from all four corners of the
earth. lə hér ---yekda in whatever
direction. həmú ---yek everybody. ləwə̀
béwlawə from then on, thenceforth.
léwlawə on the other hand; meanwhile.
lə ---yekəwə...lə ---yek-i tïrəwə on the
one hand...and on the other. lə...béw---wə
with the exception of... With neg.: only.
lém---w ʔəw---i on either side of, around.
la-i, bə la-i...əwə in the opinion of.
lam wayə I am of the opinion that... bə
---i mïnəwə in my opinion. ʔəmdərsém
--- zor xóšə I think, this lesson is very
nice. šutít --- baštïrə yan kalék? do
you prefer watermelon or cantelōupe? mïn
ʔəwóm bə laəwə gïrïŋtïrə this is more important as far as I am concerned. bə ---i
xótəwə dərwíšit you consider yourself a
dervish. --- bə --- sideways. la-i, lə
la-i, bə la-i...da beside, next to, near.
hər bə ---ya náče it doesn't even come
near it. la-i at the place of, at, with.
---i xótan at your office. ʔəčinə láy
we'll go to his place (home, business, etc.)
nəxtek lám řá ʔəwəsta he would stand with
me for a while. la b.: ...y layə s.th. to
be at the side of, with s.o.; to have s.th.
la bïrdïn to remove; to abolish. ləsər la
bïrdïn to carry to one side, remove. la
čún to go away. lá čo go away! la dán
to put aside, remove; to change course,
follow a different course. lə ře la dán
to go off the road; to digress from one's
path. xoy lə...la dan to avoid s.th.
pewístə ʔéw nusərè xoy lə wušə-i begané ---
da it is necessary for that writer to avoid
the use of foreign words. la bə la k. to

put s.th. in proper order; to settle, dispose of. čak lə...k. bə láda to buckle down to...

لا به لا كردن labəlakïrdín disposing (of a problem)

لادى ladé countryside

لافاو lafáw flood. ---ek-i zór a big flood

لاك lak carcass, corpse

لالانەوه lə...lalanəwé (lale-) to pray passionately to

لاله زار laləzár garden of flowers

لالش lalíš Lalish (place name)

لم lam name of the letter l. ---i qəléw velarized ḻ (ل). ---i zəʕíf plain l̄ (ل)

لا په ره lapəř̌é page

لا ره لا ره larəlaré reeling from side to side, staggering (n.)

لا رو له نجه larulənjé graceful gait

لارى lař̌é path paralleling road

لاشه lašé corpse; dead body

لاو law youth, young man. pl. lawán youth, youths

لاواز lawáz feeble, weak; thin. bir-i -́- a poor idea

لاولاو lawláw (a flower)

لايه ن layén object; matter; item. see also ləlayén

لازم lazím (foll. by subjunct.) necessary. -́-ə qaʔɪd-i fɪrqə̀ hazírbe it is necessary for the division commander to be present

لــــى　　le (preverb, used in verbal phrases) from (see under verb with which it occurs). (alternate form of prep. lə, which see.)

لــى بوردن　　leburdín forgiving (n.), forgiveness. dawá-i leburdíni kírd he asked for forgiveness

لــــيدان　　ledán striking, beating (n.)

لــى دوان　　ledwán conversation, talk. ---ek-i donkišotí a Quixotic argument

لــــيفه　　lefé quilt

ليك　　lek (contr. of lə yek) together

ليكدانهوه　　lekdanəwé interpretation; explanation; deep study, deliberation

ليكولينهوه　　lekolinəwé discussion; careful study, research

لى تهرمان　　leqəwmán misfortune, disaster

لى تهرماو　　leqəwmáw distressed (with misfortune), bereaved

ليشاو　　lešáw great flow; down-pour

لــيو　　lew lip

لــيژ　　lež steep

لــــــ　　lə (le occurs with pron. suff. as object: léman = lə ʔemé) from; in, at. lə...da in. lə...əwe from. leré(da) in this place, here; leréwə from here. lə séda bist twenty percent. ---bəɣá(wə) from Baghdad. ---zístan(da) in winter. ---sərətá-i maŋəkə-i tír at the beginning of next month. In comparisons: than. ləwə gəwrətírə it is bigger than that. žapón lə ʔeme peš kəwtúwə Japon is more advanced than we are. freq. combines with nouns, etc. to form compd. prps., as lə naw within, lə bín beside, etc.

لــهمانه　　ləmané of these

100

له مه و به ر	léməwbèr ago, before now; previously
له مه ودوا	léməwdwà from now on
له بابه ت	lə babət...əwə concerning, about. see babét
له به ر	ləbér in front of, before; because of. --- dərgá in front of the door. --- ʔəwé because of that, therefore. --- čí why? --- əwé-i since, because. --- k. to put on, wear. --- dém before, in the presence of
له به ر هه لسان	ləbərhəlsán standing erect, standing up straight (n.)
له د ايك بوون	lədaykbún birth; birthday
له گه ل	ləgél...(da) with, together with. --- bĭradérekya ču bò bazár he went with a friend of his to the bazaar. ləgəl ʔəwéša in addition to that also, further-more. With two objects where the second object is a pron. suffix. denoting actor: to be talking to s.o. ləgəl ké ta who are you addressing? ləgəl mĭnyéti he is talking to me .
له لايه ن ....وه	lə layén...əwə (denotes the agent in a pass. constr.) by. --- kéwə nerrawi by whom were you sent?
له ناو بردن	lənawbĭrdín elimination, annihilation
له ناو چوون	lənawčún nonexistence; destruction, de-vastation
له نجه	lənjé dance, dancing
له په و ر وو	ləpəwřú face down
له قله ق	ləqléq stork
له ره	ləré quiver, vibration; melodies
له رينه وه	lərinəwé (lər-) to shake, quiver (intr.)

101

لەرز   lə́rz   shivering, quivering; quaking (with fear) (n.)

لەرزین   lərzín (lərz-)   to shiver, tremble, quake (intr.)

لەرزوك   lərzók   quivering, shaking (adj.)

لەرزوتا   lə̀rzutá   malaria

لەڕ   lə̌ř   thin; weak

لەسەر   ləsér   on, on top of; on the account of, at the expense of; according to, on the authority of. štəkánĭm --- zəwí dawə I put my things on the ground. --- xó slowly

لەش   lə́š   body. xwə́n lə lə́šda ʔəžetəwə blood comes alive again in our veins

لەشكر   ləškĭr   army; troops

لەت   lə́t (in cpds.)   half-

لطيف   lətíf (abbrev. of ʕəbdĭllətíf)   Latif (m.p.n.)

لەوڕ   ləwə̌ř   grazing, pasturing (of sheep, etc.)

لەوڕاندن   ləwəřandĭn (ləwəřen-)   to graze, put to pasture

لەوح   ləwh̲   tablet, slate

بەلەزەت   ləzə́t: bə--- delicious. bə --- k. to make s.o. delicious

ليته   lité   slime

ليتر   lítr   liter (of)

لوا   liwá   county; liwa, province (one of the administrative units of Iraq)

ليژنه   ližné   committee; commission

لباد   lĭbád   a small rug made of felt

لج   lĭč   lip. --- həl̲ qurčandĭn (qurčen-)

	to bite one's lips; to pout (in disapproval)
لفکـه	lĭfké wash-towel (used for scrubbing when taking a bath)
پیکه وه لکاندن	lĭkandĭn (lken-) p̀ekəwə to stick s.th. together; to unite; bring close together
لـم	lĭm sand
لـرفه	lĭrfé sweep, drive (n.)
لـوبیا	lobyá black-eyed peas
لـوکه	loké cotton
لو لوو هاتم هاتم	l̀olo hátĭm "Lolo" (Kurdish folk song)
لوته نته چی	loqəntəčí innkeeper
لـوری	lorí Lurish
لـوو	lu cyst; tumor
لـوله توپ	lulətóp canon
لـوراندن	lurandĭn (luren-) to howl (wolf, jackal)
لـوره لـور	lurəlúr howling (n.) (of dogs, wolves, etc.)
لـووت	lút nose
لـوتکه	lutké peak (of a mountain); hill
لـووتقنج	lutqĭnj snub-nosed
لـبنان	lʊbnán, lıbnán Lebanon
لـبنانی	lʊbnaní Lebanese
لـوتف	lʊtf gentleness; kindness, benevolence. --- ləgəl...da b. to be kind to s.o. lútfi ləg̅éla buwə he has been kind to him
لـوتفـن	lútfən please (in requests)

103

م ‎ m

میلادی	m. = miladí A.D.
ماچ کردن	mač kiss. --- k. to kiss. déstĭt mač ʔəkəm I kiss your hand (in entreaty, etc.)
ماد	mad Mede; the Medes
مادی	madí, maddí materialistic, material (as opp. to spiritual). zïruf-i -́- material circumstances
ماف	máf right (n.), rights
مایس	maís May (month)
ماکینه	makiné machine
مالوم	malúm rabbi
مال	mál¹ house; household; wife (polite). mál̄tan bə qúř gire may your house be covered with mud! (curse). --- bə --- house by house, from house to house. ---i ʔewé mïnyan bóči what does your wife want with me? máḻəwə (as obj. of prep.) home. lə maləwéyə he is at home
مال	mál² money; wealth; property. ---i sïpí bo řož-i řəš save for a rainy day (prov.)
هه لمالین	malín (maḻ-) to throw, cast. həl --- to remove. řa --- to sweep out; to drive away
مال ویرانی	maḻweraní disaster, blow, calamity
مام	mám (paternal) uncle; (title of respect for older males)
مامو ستا	mamostá, mamwəstá master craftsman; teacher, professor; (often used as title of respect)
ماموه ستا	mamwəsta = mamostá teacher
مان	mán¹ (men-) to remain, stay, be left;

to continue to exist, remain alive. Neg.: to be no more Neg., replacing bun in a verbal phrase: no longer. ta máwə as long as he is alive. řa --- to pause. --- ləsər... to follow, maintain, continue (a practice)

مـــان mán² remaining (n.); existence; subsistence

مانـــا maná = məʕná meaning (n.). bə həmú ---yek in the full sense of the word

مانـــدو mandú tired, weary. --- k. to tire, exhaust s.o.

ماندویتی mandwetí tiredness, weariness, fatigue

مانـــوه manəwé (men-) to remain, stay, stay behind, be left behind; to remain (bo: as the lot of). čénd řož ʔəmenítəwə lə slemaní? how long will you be staying in Sul.?

مانگـــر mangír obstinate, stubborn

مانگ maŋ moon; month. ---i čwardé the full moon; (often used as symbol of a beautiful girl)

مانگانـه maŋané monthly payment; salary

مانگا maŋgá cow

مـــار már snake

مارکـه marké mark; trade-mark

مارماسی marmasí eel

مارشال maršál marshal

مارت mart March

ماسی masí fish

ماست mast yoghurt

ماستاو mastáw (a drink consisting of mast and water)

ماستفروش	mastfroš yoghurt-seller
مات كردن	mat k. to keep s.o. silent
ماتـم	matém funeral
ماتـى	matí dejection
ماوه	mawé[1] period, time; a while. bə ---yek-i kém in a short time
ماوه	mawé[2] chance, opportunity. --- d. to permit, allow
ماوه	mawé[3] remainder. lə ---i maŋəkéda by the end of the month
ماوسوله	mawsulé coldness. ---i zïstán the cold of winter
مايه	mayé essence; source; factor; cause; capital
مى	me female
مىباز	mebáz heterosexual male
مىرد	merd husband
مىرگ	merg meadow
مىش	meš fly, flies
مىشوله	mešulé mosquito
مىشومەگەز	mešuməgéz insects
مىشك	mešïk brain
مىرژ	mewúž raisins
مىز	mez table
مـىـژ	mež a long time. lə -´-ə... it has been a long time since...
مىژوو	mežú history
مىژونوس	mežunús historian

مأمور   məʔmír (govt.) official, civil servant

مه عاش   məʕáš salary

مه عاشخور   məʕašxór employee

معدن   məʕdén metal

مه عنا   məʕná, maná meaning, signification. ---y číyə what does it mean?

مه نه وى   mə̀ʕnəwí spiritual (as opp. to material)

مه به س   məbés intention, purpose; aim, goal; meaning. mïn hər řïzgarbun-i sïzam la -´-bu my only purpose was to save Siza. -´-ït čıyə lə saḻan-i šwári? what do you mean by saḻaní šwari? --- lə...ʔəwébuə (foll. by ṣubjunct.) the purpose in...has been to

مه چو ك   məčék wrist; forearm

مه چه كئه ستور   məčekʔəstúr having powerful arms

منهسوم   məfhúm concept, notion

مه كه ر   mégər unless, if not

مهدى   məhdí Mahdi (m.p.n.)

محلسى   məhellí local

مه حكه م   məhkém strong, powerful, well-fortified

محكمه   məhkəmé court (of law)

محمود   məhmí[d] Mahmoud (m.p.n.)

مه جه له   məjəllé magazine

مجيد   məjí[d] Majid (m.p.n.)

مجلس   məjlís council, mejlis. ---i bələdıyé city council

مجمع   məjméʕ council; academy

مه جول   məjoḻ Majol (m.p.n.)

107

مه‌کینه	məkiné	engine; machine
مکتب	məktéb	school. ---i ʔewarán night school
مه‌ل	mél	bird; water-birds
مه‌لا	məlá	Mulla (religious title given to men well-versed in Islamic religion; title precedes name)
مه‌لاژن	məlažín	mullah's wife
مه‌له‌	məlé	swimming (n.). --- k. to swim
مه‌لاس دان	məlás:	--- d. to conceal, hide, hide in silence
مه‌لکه‌ندی	mèlkəŋí	Melkendi (a quarter of Sul.)
مه‌مله‌که‌ت	məmləkét	kingdom, country
منون	məmnún	obliged, grateful. --- k. to please, gratify
منع	mənʕ	forbidding (n.)
مه‌نجه‌ل	mənjél	pot
مقناطیس	məqnatís	magnetism
مه‌ردانه‌	mərdané	manfully, boldly
مه‌ردوم	mərdúm	person, human being, man
مه‌ره‌که‌ب	mərəkəb	ink
مه‌رگ	mérg¹	death
مه‌رگ	mərg²	(green) pasture
مه‌رحه‌با	mérhəba	hello. --- le k. to say "hello" to s̄.o.
مه‌ریوان	məriwán	Mariwan (a Kurdish district in Iran)
مه‌رج	mərj	condition, provision
مرکـز	mərkéz	center, headquarters; capital (of province)

108

مەرقەد   mərqéd   mausoleum; shrine

مەر   məř   sheep

مەرمەرر   məřméř   marble

مصـدر   məsdér   infinitive

مەسەلە   məsəlé   question, problem; matter

مەسیحی   məsihí   Christian; Christianity

مصـرف   məsríf   bank

مەست   məst   intoxicated, drunk; exhilarated

مەشهور بە   məšhúr bə   famous for

مەشق   méšïq   drill (n.), exercise (military, etc. etc.)

مەشق گاە   məšïqgah   drill grounds, parade grounds (mil.)

مەسلەحەت   məsləhét   interest, advantage, benefit

مەتعم   mətˤém   restaurant

مەترسی   mətïrsí   danger; fear

مەتر   mətr   meter

مەولەوی   məwləwí   Mawlawi (a famous Kurdish poet)

مولود   məwlúd   mawlud, anniversary of the Prophet's birthday

مولود نامە   mèwlu[d]namé   Mawludname, a eulogy recited on the occasion of the Prophet's birthday

موضوعی   məwzuˤí   objective

مەیدان   məydán   square (of city, etc.)

مەینەتی   məynətí   misery; disaster

مەزە   məzé   appetizers, hors d'oeuvres

مەزەندە   məzəndé   a guess, estimate. --- k. bə... to estimate s.th. at, to be ...

مه‌زن	məzi̇́n great; colossal
دا مه‌زراندن	da məzrandí̇n (məzren-) to establish, set up; to appoint, employ s.o. (bə: as)
ميكانيكى	mikaniki̇́ mechanical. bə šewèyek-i --- in a mechanical fashion, mechanically
ميكرفون	mikrofón microphone
ميـلادى	miladi̇́ A.D.
ميلله‌ت	millét people, nation. hĭkumèt-i -́-u bə hò-i -́-əwə government of the people and by the people
ميللـى	milli̇́ national; of the people. čin-i -́- Chinese People's Republic
مينه	miné a kind of flower
مـــير	mi̇́r prince, emir (title formerly given to princes of a ruling house). mìr-i mirán prince of princes
ميريه‌تى	mireti̇́ emirate, princedom
ميرى	miri̇́ government
ميرنشين	mìmɪši̇́n capital, seat of a principality
ميرزا	mirzá Mirza (title formerly given to laymen who could read and write; usually precedes the first name). --- qadĭr Mirza Qadir
ميسر	mi̇́sɪr, mĭsi̇́r Egypt
ميوان	miwán guest, visitor
ميوانداري	miwandari̇́ hospitality
ميوانـى	miwani̇́ visiting (n.). ʔəci̇́n bo --- they go visiting
ميوه	miwé fruit
ميزانيه	mizanɪyé budget (finance)
محمد	mĭhəmméd Mohammed

110

میکــروب	mĭkrób microbe; germ
مـل	mĭl neck. bə --- yəkda kəwtĭn to fall on e.o. bo (naw)...---nán (ne-) to betake o.s. to..., follow one's nose to
مل به رز	mĭlbérz stiff-necked, with head erect, i.e., fearlessly
ملمتر	mĭlimétr millimeter
ملوانكه	mĭlwaŋké necklace
مليار	mĭlyár billion
مليون	mĭlyón million. mĭlyonəhá millions
من	mĭn I
منــال	mĭnál, mĭndál child
منالـى	mĭnalí childhood
مقياس	mĭqyás measurement, measure, standard
مــــر	mĭr hen
مراوى	mĭrawí duck
مرد ن	mĭrdĭn¹ (mr-) to die
مرد ن	mĭrdĭn² dying, death
مرد وو	mĭrdú dead
به مرد وبى	mĭrduí lifelessness. bə --- dead, lifeless
مريشك	mĭrišĭk chicken
مروف	mĭróv man, person
مروفايه تى	mĭrovayətí humanity
مرواری	mĭrwarí pearl(s)
مسك	mĭsĭk mouse
مست	mĭst palm

مصطفى	mĭstəfá	Mustafa (m.p.n.)
مستر	mĭstér	Mister
مسیو	mĭsyó	monsieur
مســو	mĭsú	handle (of dagger, etc.)
مشه مش	mĭšemĭš	labored breathing through the nose
مسكه ری	mĭzgərí	copper-smithery
مزكه وت	mĭzgéwt	mosque. ---i gəwré the Great Mosque (in Sul.)
مزل	mĭzíl	dill (taste)
نـــژ	mĭž	a sip; a whiff of smoke. --- lə...d. to take a puff on (a cigarette)
مـژده	mĭždé, muždé	good news, glad tidings
مژین	mĭžín (mž-)	to suck
میان دواو	mɪyandwáw	Miyandoab (city in Iranian Kurdistan)
مررر بو نه وه	lə...moř b.əwé	to stare (with anger) at s.o.
مو سیقا	mosiqá	music
موز	moz	banana(s)
	mr-	see mĭr-
مـــو	mí	hair (of animals)
مو چه	mučé	salary, wages
مو چه خور	mùčəxór	salaried person; (govt.) official
موو سل	muṣíl	Mosul
مو فق	muwəfféq	successful
معاملـــه	muʕaməlé	treatment, dealing with
معارض	muʕaríz	opponent

112

معلم   muꜥəllím   teacher

موعيشه   muꜥišé   salary

معتدل   muꜥtədíl   moderate, mild

موچركه   mučĭrké   tremor, shivering; nervous ex-
citement. ---y pya hatĭn   to tremble,
shiver (with emotion). ---m pya   yet
I'm trembling

مدەت   muddét   interval of time, period, time

مدتق   mudəqqíq   auditor

مهندس   muhəndís   engineer

مهم   muhím   important

محامى   muḥamí   lawyer

محەرەم   muḥərém   Moharam (m.p.n.)

ملكدار   mʊlkdár   landlord, property owner

معكن   mʊmkín   possible

مناقەشه   mʊnaqəšé   debate. --- k. to debate (a
question)

مقاطعه   mʊqatəꜥé   region, province

مراجعه   mʊrajəꜥé   review

مستعمره   mʊstəꜥməré   colony

مشترى   mʊštɪří   customer

موصلاوى   mʊsḻawí   of Mosul; a Mosulite

موسولمان   mʊsʊlmán   Muslim

موسولمانى   mʊsʊlmaní   Islam

متصرف   mʊtəsəríf   governor (of a liwa)

متوسطه   mʊtəwəssĭté   intermediate (school)

موافقه   mʊwafəqé   agreement

مياوانن   myawanín (mawen-)   to miaw

ن n

نائب	naʔíb delegate; parliament member
نائومید بوون	lə...naʔumed b. to have no hope of, for, despair of
نائومیدی	naʔumedí despair; despondency, hopelessness
ناچار	načár helpless to do otherwise; forced by the situation. --- b. (kə...) to have no alternative (but to...)
به ناچاری	način: bə --- helpless to do otherwise, of necessity, inexorably
نادی	nadí club, society
نادر	nadír Nadir (m.p.n.)
ناهه موار	nahəmwár unhappy; unfortunate
به ناحه ق	nahéq: bə --- inequitably, unjustly
ناحه ز	nahéz inimical; unfriendly; hostile
ناحیه	nahiyé 'nahiya' (in Iraqi political structure, subdivision of a qaḍāʔ, roughly equivalent to a county)
نالاندن	nalandín¹ (nalen-) to groan, moan (with pain, weariness, etc.)
نالاندن	nalandín² groaning; complaining (n.)
نالـــه	nalé moaning, groaning (n.)
ناماقوولی	námaqulì unreasonableness; nonsense, stupid talk
نامه	namé letter, message
نــان	nan¹ bread; loaf of bread. --- xwardín to eat a meal, eat, dine
نــان	nan² (ne-) to put; to touch s.th. to (bə...əwə) s.th. da --- to put, place s.th. down; to set up, establish; to start, launch; to use, utilize; to appoint;

to draw up, draft; to propose; to open
up (shop); to prepare (food); to regard,
consider s.o. (bə: as). štəkánĭm ləsər
zəwí dà na I placed my things on the ground.
čéstĭm bo le na I prepared food for him.
heštá dukáni da nénawə he hasn't opened up
his shop yet. nəxšə́y bo dá ʔəne he lays
a plan for it. da nrán (pass.) to begin,
start. pe lə...--- to admit, acknowledge,
confess. péləwə nĭràwə kə... it has been
acknowledged that...

نانه وا nanəwá baker

نانه وه nanəwə́ affecting; bringing about

نان که ر nankə́r baker. ---i malán person who
assists various households in their bread-
making

نان کویری nankwerí ungratefulness, ingratitude

نان خوارد ن nanxwardín meal. ---i niwəřó lunch

نارد ن nardín (ner-) to send, to forward; to
submit. --- bə dwai...da, ---...henán
to send for...

نارد نه وه nardnəwə́ (ner-) to send back (bo: to)

نارینج narénj citron

ناره زایی narəzaí displeasure; resentment

نارره وا nařəwá inaccuracy, inappropriateness.
bə --- inaccurately, improperly

ناسین nasín (nas-) to know, be acquainted with
s.o. nénasraw unknown

ناشیرین naširin not sweet; unpleasant

ناشیرینی naširiní unpleasantness; foul language

ناته واو nátəwaw incomplete; deficient, not good
(people)

ناو naw¹ name; (good) name; fame. nàwĭt
číyə? what is your name? xan geldi --́-
someone called Khan Geldi. bə ---ⁱi...(əwə)

115

by the name of; in the name of; on the pretext of. bə ---i xómewə in my own name, on behalf of myself. --- bïrdïn to mention. nawbráw the above-mentioned. --- henán to mention, name, speak about. --- nán to name, call s.o. s.th. (bə naw-i...əwə: after). ʔəmhalé --- ʔənre čí? what would you call this condition? bə nàw-i sleman pašáwə --- nra it was named after Sulayman Pasha

ناو   naw² inside, inner part. bə ---; lə ---, ---...da, lə---...da inside, within, in, among. --- šár inside the city. lə --ya inside it. wa gəyštə ---yan he is now arriving among them. ---...əwə in, into. lə --- bïrdïn to wipe out, eliminate, exterminate. lə ---da b. to exist. lə nawdáyə there is, there exists. lə ---da níyə it does not exist. lə --- čun to fall apart, disintegrate, cease, to exist, disappear. lə ---da həl gïrtïn to annihilate

ناو   naw³ = nawčə́ area, region, district; place, vicinity

ناوبانگ   nàwbáŋ fame. bə --- famous

ناوبازار   nawbazár the principal bazaar, the main shopping area

ناوچ   nawčə́ region, district, area; province

ناوچەوان   nawčəwán forehead

ناودار   nawdár well-known, famous

ناودەرکردن   nawdér k. to gain renown, become famous

ناوەندی   nawəndí intermediate

ناوەراست   nawəřást middle, center. řožhəlàt-i -- the Middle East

ناوشار   nawšár downtown

ناوخو   nawxó local; domestic

ناخ   nax roots; the inner part; the very depths (of)

ناخوش	naxóš unpleasant. bə...--- b. to be unpleasant for. to slemaní̵t pe --- níyə? don't you find Sulaimania unpleasant?
نایاب	nayáb excellent, very good; rare, unattainable
نایلون	naylón nylon; plastic
نازدار	nazdár darling, beloved; pampered
نیر	ner male
نیرباز	nerbáz heterosexual (woman)
نیرگس	nergís narcissus (flower)
نیرینه	neriné male; man
نیرو	nerú force (military). ---i həwaí air force
له نیوان	newán: lə --- between
نه ... ه	né...né, né...we né neither...nor. ---nizík --- dúr neither near nor far
نه؟	né? no; nay, more than that
نه عنه ع	nəʕnéʕ mint; peppermint
نه به ز	nəbéz invincible
نه بوون	nəbún non-existence; lack (of)
نه بوونسی	nəbuní non-existence; lack; poverty
نه فام	nəfám irrational, not sensible
نه فامی	nəfamí ignorance
نه فی	nəfí exiled
نه گبه ت	nəgbét unfortunate, unlucky. ʔemə-i --- ! unlucky us!
نه هاته دی	nəhatnədí frustration, thwarting (of s.th.)
نه هیشتن	nəheštín complete destruction, annihilation

117

نه جات بوون له	nəjat b. lə to be rescued from
نه جیب	nəjíb noble, highminded, magnanimous
نه ک	nək not, and not. --- ləbər híč štek and not for any reason. Foll. by subjunct.: lest. --- (tənhá)...bélku not (only)... but rather...
نه مر	nəmír immortal
نه نسک	nénïk father's mother
نه قابه	nəqabé trade union
نقیب	nəqíb head of a union
نه راندن	nərandín (nəren-) to roar
نه رم	nérïm soft, smooth
نه رم ونیان	nèrmunɪyán soft and smooth
نه رم ونول	nərmunól soft and smooth; tender
نه سرین	nəsrín a kind of flower; Nasrin (f.p.n.)
نه ته وایه تی	nətəwayətí national racial
نه ته وه	nətəwé people; race; nation. --- yək-gïrtokán the United Nations
نه ته وه ی	nətəweí national(istic); nationalism
نه توانین	nətwanín inability, incapacity
نه و ع	nəwʕ kind, type. zór ---i həyə it has many varieties
دا نه وواندن	nəwandín (nəwen-): da --- to bring down, lower. sər da --- to bow the head (in servility)
نه وه	nəwé offspring, descendant; generation
نه وه د	nəwéd, nəwét ninety
نه وه ک ... به لکو	néwək...bélku not only...but also
نه وروز	nəwřóz New Year

118

نەوت	nəwt oil; gasoline
نەوزاد	nəwzád Nawzad (m.p.n.)
نەخیر	néxer no, not at all
نەخوش	nəxóš sick, sick man; patient. pyaw-i --- "The Sick Man of Europe"
نەخوشی	nəxošī́ sickness, illness, disease
نەخوشخانه	nəxošxané hospital
نەخشه	nəxšə́ map; plan; guidelines
نەختیك	néxtek a little; somewhat
نەخویندەوار	nəxwendəwár unlettered; illiterate
نەخویندەواری	nəxwendəwarí ignorance; illiteracy
نەزانی	nəzaní ignorance
نەژاد	nəžád origin; stock
نیگار	nigár portrait, picture
نینوك	ninók fingernail, nail
نیسان	nisán April
نیشان	nišán target. --- d. to show, manifest. --- šīkandīn target shooting
نیشانه	nišané sign, mark, imprint
نیشتەجی	ništəjé habitation; residence. --- k. to settle s.o. (in a place)
نیشتگه	ništgə́ settlement
نیشتمان	ništīmán country; fatherland
نیشتمانی	ništīmaní national, of the country, patriotic
نیشتمان پەروەر	nɪštīmanpərwér patriot
نیشتمان پەروەری	nɪštīmanpərwərí patriotism

119

نیشتن   niští̃n, nɪští̃n (niš-) to sit; to lie, settle down. da --- to sit down; to reside (lə: in). --- lə ... to alight, settle down on

نیشتنه‌وه   ništnəwə́ (niš-) to land, to alight (birds, planes)

نیو   nı́w half. --- hoqqá half a hoqqa. niw is used foll. n.⁻, while niwə́ 'half' is used independently

نیوان   niwán: lə ---i...(da) in the midst of, in, among. lə ---...əwə from among

نیوه   niwə́ half (used figuratively; see niw). ---i gèlə it is half of the nation

نیوه‌رو   niwəřó midday; noon

نیوه‌شه‌و   niwəšə́w midnight

نظام الدین   nizaməddı́n Nizam Al-Din (m.p.n.)

نهینی   nı̈henı́ secret (adj.)

نکول کردن   nı̈kul-i...k. to deny s.th.

نم   nı̈m fine moisture; dampness

نمایش   nı̈mayı́š exercises and athletic events; parade; procession

نمونه   nı̈munə́ sample, model, pattern, example

نقه کردن   nı̈qə k. to utter, say s.th.

نقوم بون   nı̈qúm b. to be sunk, sink (intr.)

نرخ   nı̈rx cost, price; value. bə hər -́-ek at any cost. bə --- valuable

نرخدار کردن   nı̈rxdar k. to value, esteem highly

نزا   nı̈zá lə invocation, calling on (God)

نزار   nı̈zár pasture, meadow

نزیک   nı̈zı́k near, close by. lə́m---ə̀ in this vicinity. lə́m ---anə̀da in the next few

120

days. (lə...)--- b.əwé ,to be near, come
close to s.th. --- ḳəwtín to come near,
approach. lə...xīstīnəwə to move s.th.
closer to...

نزیکه‌ی   nīzikéy about, approximately. --- dé
mīlyonə it is about ten million

نـزم   nīzīm low

نسبت   nɪsbét relationship; comparison. bə ---
relatively

nɪšt- see also ništ-

نیابی   nɪyabí representative, parliamentary (govt.)

نیاز   nɪyáz intention. ---īm wábu it was my
intention to... bə ---ek-i xawén with
good intent

نی یه   nīyə is not. see bun

نزام ، نظام   nɪzám system, order

نـــو   no nine

نـــوك   nok¹ chickpeas

نـــوك   nok² d. to kneel

نـوكه‌ر   nokér servant

نوره   noré turn. ---i mīnə it's my turn

نوشی   noš-i gyán here's to your health! (toast)

نـوره‌م   nowém ninth

نویه‌مین   noyəmín = nowém ninth

نوزده   nozdé nineteen

نوزده‌هه‌م   nozdəhém nineteenth

نـــوك   nuk point. ---i xənjér the point of a
dagger

نورساندن (به)   nusandín (nusen-) to stick, press s.th.
(bə...əwə: to); to move s.th. close (bə...
əwə: to)

121

نووســـر	nusér writer, author
نو سین	nusín[1] (nus-) to write
نو سین	nusín[2] writing (n.); writings
نو سراو	nusráw written; written material; publication
نو ستن	nustín, nʊstín (nu-) to sleep
نو ستن وخو اردن	nustínuxwardín room and board
نــووزه	nuzé a moan; a very faint sound
نفـــوس	nʊfús people, population (of a city, etc.)
نوکته	nʊkté joke
نوکته باز	nʊktəbáz joker, comedian
نقطه	nʊqté point; item
نقـــول	nʊqúḻ candy, sweets
نقوم کردن	nʊqʊm k. to inundate, flood s.th.
نوقورچ	nʊqúrč a pinch. --- gĭrtín to pinch
	nʊst- see nust-
نوخشه	nʊxšé good fortune. ---š bĭbe lə... we (I) wish the same good fortune for... ---šbe lə həmí bradəràn I wish the same good fortune to all our friends
نواندن	nwandín (nwen-) to represent; to look like, appear as; to appeal, have appeal (for s.o.)
نواندوه	nwandú displayed
نـــوى	nwe new. lə --- anew, again. sér lə --- all over again
نــوین	nwen bedding
نوینـه ر	nwenér representative. ---an-i sɪyasí- dərəwə foreign diplomats
نـــویژ	nwež prayer. --- k. to pray

پ p

پـا	pa leg
پاچ	pač pick-ax
پاداش	padaš reward; prize
پاك	pak clean; sacred, holy. --- k. to clean; to peel (fruit). --- k.əwə́ to clean, cleanse, wash; to clean out; to purify
پاكانـه	pakanə́ oath. --- k. to swear
پاكستان	pakĭstán pakistan
پاك كردنـه وه	pakkĭrdnəwə́ cleaning, polishing (n.)
پاك وتـه ميز	pakutəmíz clean and tidy
پاله وان	paləwán athlete
پال	pál side; foot; support. lə -́-əwə while sitting still, unmoving. --- d.əwə́ to recline, lean against. --- pewə nán to push, impel; to prompt, induce (s.o. to do s.th.). ləsər --- xĭstín to make s.o. lie down. ...dánə ---... to ascribe s.th. to s.th.
پان	pán wide; broad. --- k. to widen
پاندان	pandán fountain pen
پانتول	pantól trousers
پانـزه	panzə́ fifteen
پاپـور	papóř ship
پار	pár last year. bə həmí-i sal-i -́- all last year
پاراستن	parastín (parez-) to protect (lə: from)
پاراشـوت	parašút combination of six and five (dice)
پارچه	parčə́ part, portion

123

پاریزەر	parezér	lawyer
پاریزگار	parezgár	protector, guardian
پاریزگاری	parezgarí	protection, defence. --- k. to protect, defend
پاره	paré	money
پاره لیدان	pareledán	coinage, minting of money
پارلمان	parləmán	parliament
پاروش	paróš	vehemence
پارسەک	parsék	beggar
پارتی	partí	(political) party
پارو	parú	morsel
پاررانەوه	pařanəwé[1] (paře-): lə...---kə, bo ʔəwə-t... (foll. by subjunct.) to beg, entreat... to (do s.th.)	
پاررانەوه	pařanəwə[2] lə	supplication, request of s.o.
پاساری	pasarí	sparrow
پاسەوانی	pasəwaní	surveillance; guard. ---ek-i zóri bo dá nawə he assigned him a large guard
پاش	paš	after. pášan afterwards. --- ʔəwé after that, then. lə pášа afterwards. --- ʔəwə-i (foll. by subjunct.) after (conj.). ləməw --- from now on. --- kəwtïn ṭo fall behind; to be backward --- xïstïn to retard, delay
پاشا	pašá	(title follows name) pasha; king; ruler, governor; king (cards). məhmu ---i babán Mahmoud Pasha of the Bābans
پاشەل	pašél	lame, cripple
پاشەل	pašél	part of cloak or gown beneath the knees
پاشەروژ	pašəřóž	future

پاشه و پاش   pašəwpaš backwards. --- gəřanəwə́ (gəře-) to retrace one's steps; to retreat

پاشین   pašı́n final

پاشكه و تور   paškəwtú backward; underdeveloped

پاشكه و توریی   paškəwtuı́ backwardness

پاشماوه   pašmawə́ left-over, remnant, remains

پاص   pas̱ bus

پایه   payə́ column; degree or level of progress

پایه به رز   payəbə́rz eminent, majestic, great

پاییز   payı́z autumn

پایته خت   paytəxt capital (city)

پــی   pe[1] foot; measurement, standard. bə́m ---yə̀ by such and such an amount; in this manner. bə ---i according to. bə ---i ḥsab according to calculations. lə --- náw-i...da for the sake of, for, because of. --- kán (kə-) to hit, shoot s.o. lə --- k. to put on (shoes). postaləkanı̆t lə pet kı̆rd? did you put your boots on? --- lə...nán to step on s.th.; to admit to s.th. kuřəké pe le na the boy admitted it (or: stepped on it). kəsiš nı́yə pe ləwə nénet kə... there is no one who will not admit that... bə ---wə řa wəstán to stand on one's feet. xı̆stnə žer --- to step on, tread on, trample

پــی   pe[2] to (alternate form of the preposition bə: bə is used with a following object which is either a noun or an independent pronoun, while pe is used in all other cases. Thus: bo tó ʔəl̲em = pét ʔəl̲em "I say to you/I tell you." Entries containing a prep. phrase with bə... accordingly imply pe under the conditions stated above. pe is also used independently, that is, not alternating with bə before nouns, and in such cases is entered as pe. pe in this independent form is used to give certain verbs causative meaning, as ʔiš bo to ʔəkəm "I work for you" and ʔišit pe ʔəkəm "I put you to work.") pe b. to be on a person; to have on one's person. dəftérim péə I have my notebook with me. see also péda, pek, péwə, pya

پیچ   peč winding (n.); curve. --- k. to roll (cigarettes)

پیچان   pečán (peč-) to fold; to wrap

پیچەوانه   pečəwané reverse, opposite. bə ---i ʔémewə in opposition to this, conversely. bə ---əwə on the contrary

پیچ وپەنا   pečupəná zigzags; circumlocution; equivocation

پێغەمبەر   peɣəmbér = peɣəmmér prophet

پێغەمەر   peɣəmmér prophet

پێك   pek (= bə + yək; verbal particle) together. --- hatin to be set up, established, formed; to form, constitute (lə...; s.th.). --- henán to form, establish s.th.

پێكەنین   pekənín laughing (n.), laughter. ---ek-i bə kul hearty laughter

پێكەوه   pékəwə (=bə + yək + -əwə; adverb) together. ʔəhméw ʕəlím --- di I saw Ahmad and Ali together. --- b. to be together, be one

پێكهاتن   pekhatín formation

پێكهێنان   pekhenán creation, establishment

پێلاو   peláw shoes

پێلو   pelú eyelid

پی مەڕه   peməřə́ spade

پیناو   penáw sacrifice. lə ---i...da for the cause of, on behalf of

پینج   penj five

پنجەر	penjǝ́r window
یینج شەمە	penjšǝmmǝ́ Thursday
پینجوین	penjwī́n Penjwin (town in Sul. Liwa)
پینوس	penú̇s pen; pencil
پیری	pére the day before yesterday
پیست	pest skin (human)
پیش	péš before; front; forward. pé̇šǝwǝ! forward! advance! lǝ -́-ǝwǝ formerly, previously. ʔémǝ řegáyek-i dúrman lǝ pé̇šǝ we have a long road ahead of us. --- kǝwtī́n to move forward, advance, progress
پیشینان	pé̇šinan the previous generations; the ancients
پیشکەوتن	peškǝwtī́n preceding, walking in front (n.); progress, advance(ment)
پیشکەتوو	peškǝwtú progressive; advanced
پیشکەوتو بوون	pèškǝwtubún the state of being prosperous; prosperity
پیشنراو	pešnĭráw suggestion, proposal
پیشنیار	pešnɪyár proposal, suggestion
پیشنیاز	pešnɪyáz suggestion, proposal. --- k. to suggest, propose
پیشــو	pešú former, previous. sǝrèk-i -́- the previous president
پیشونیان	pešunyán the previous ones; old ones; ancestors
پیشراز	peš̌wáz reception, meeting. --- k. to receive
پیشوەخت	peš̌wǝ́xt premature, untimely
پیشخستن	pešxĭstī́n advancement, development

127

پیوان   pewán measure, measurement

پیواندن   pewandín (pew-) to measure s.th.

پیوانه   pewané measurement (of length etc.).
--- k. to measure

پیوه   péwə (= bə + -əwə; prep.) in, on (trans-
lation varies acc. to verb with which it
is used). -- b. to be on, in; to have.
dú gʊlley --- bu there were two bullets
in him. ʔə́w darə̀ miwə́y ---yə that tree
has fruit on it. bə́fru tərzə́y --- bu it
was accompanied by snow and hail. --- k.
to entrap, snare. --- mán to remain on
(it). see also pya

پیویست   pewíst, pewíst necessity, requirement,
necessary. --- b. bə... to be in need
of, need. --́-bum bə ʔɪsrahə́t I needed
rest. ---y bə...həyə to need to (do
s.th.), one must... ---i bə xənjə́r həyə
he needs a dagger. --- bə...k. to be
necessary for s.o. to do s.th. -́-- bəwə
nákat kə bíleyn there is no need for us
to say... bə --- zanín to find it
necessary (to do s.th.) bə ---ĭm nə́zani
bĭčĭm bo dʊktór I didn't think it necessary to go to the doctor

پیویستی   pewɪstí need, necessity

پهلامار دان   pəlamárː lə...da --- d. to grab, seize,
clutch at; to attack

پهله   pəlé haste. ---y b. to be in a hurry.
pəlémə I'm in a hurry. --- k. to be in
a hurry. --- mə́kə don't be in a hurry!

پهلهقاژی   pələqažé desperate movement of hands and
legs

پهلوپو   pəlupó limbs; branches; arms; hands

پهله   pəlé stain, spot

پهمهیی   pəmeí pink

په نا   pəná   corner; nook; shelter, refuge. lə
--- ʔəméyə   it is behind this.   ---i be
dəŋí   muteness.   --- bïrdnə bə́r   to resort
to

په نابهر   pənabə́r   refugee

په ند   pənd¹   pun (ləsər: on); trick; maxim.   ---i
pešinán   proverb.   --- bə...d.   to play a
trick on.   bóči pə́ndït pe dam?   why did you
play a trick on me?

په ند   pənd²   advice.   --- d.   to advise

په نهان   pənhán   enigmatic, puzzling

په نیر   pəní r   cheese

په نجا   pənjá   fifty.   -́-w yək   fifty-one

په نجه   pənjə́   finger; hand.   ---i pé   toe

په نجه ره   pənjərə́   window

په نسلین   pənsïlín   penicillin

به نگ خوارد ن   pəŋ xwardïn   to be sealed up, curbed, held
in check (water; emotions, as anger, etc.)

په نگاو   pəŋáw   pool (of water)

په نگ خوارد و   pəŋxwardú   sealed up, curbed, locked up
(emotions, water, etc.)

په پو سلیمانکه   pəpú s̲lemankə́   hoopoe

پهر   pər   side

دههپه راندن   pərandïn (pəren-): lə...dər ---   to force
s.o. to evacuate..., expel s.o. from...

پهرچ دانهوه   pərčdanəwə́   refutation, rebuttal

پهرچم   pərčə́m   locks of hair; forelock

پهرداخ   pərdáx   glass, tumbler.   pərdáxek ʔaw
a glass of water

پهرده   pərdə́   curtain

په رده وکولله	pərdèwkullé	mosquito netting
په ریشان	pəresán	in danger, in critical condition; desolate. --- b. to be ruined
په ره سندن	pərə səndín (sen-)	to grow, flourish, prosper, increase
په ره سه ندن	pərəsəndín	growth, expansion
په ریخان	pərixán	Perikhan (f.p.n.)
په رست	pəríst	worshiper
په رستگا	pərístgá	temple, shrine
په رستز	pərístín (pəríst-)	to worship
په رستش	pərístíš	pious
په رله مان	pərləmán	parliament
په ر وه ر	pərwér	person who zealously supports (country, natural beauty, etc.) e.g. ništīman pərwér patriot
په روه رده کردن	pèrwərdə k.	to tend; to raise tenderly
په رژین	pəržín	fence; guarding wall, usually of thorns, etc.; bulwark
په رراندن	pəřandín (pəřen-)	to cut off, sever
په راو	pəřáw	book
په رره	pəřé	page
په رره سیلکه	pəřəselké	swallow (bird)
په ررین	pəřín (pəř-): dər --- to flee, rush out. həl --- to dance. te --- (bəsér) to pass, pass by, go across. lə...te --- to pass through...
په ررو	pəřó	cloth, wash rag
په ر پوت	pəřpút	a kind of dice game
په ر تووك	pəřtúk	booklet; pamphlet; manuscript

130

په سه ند	pəsénd commendable; proper. --- k. to approve of; to agree to; to choose, select
په ست	pəst spiritless, dejected; depressed; melancholy. lə...--- b. to be annoyed at, disgusted at
په سته ك	pəstӗk, pəsӗk felt or woolen vest
په ستی	pəstí degradation, debasement
په ستن	pəstín (pəst-) to press
په شیمان	pəšimán regretful, sorry. --- b. lə... to be regretful, sorry over
په ت	pət rope
په تی	pətí pure; unadulterated
په خش	pəxš shining; blooming
په خشان	pəxšán Pakhshan (f.p.n.)
په یام	pəyám message
په یدا	pəydá: --- b. to come into being, be created; to break out; to come along, happen along. --- k. to get, acquire
په یدابوون	pəydabún coming into being, advent
په یکه ر	pəykӗr statue; symbol
په یره و	pəyrӗw principle; teachings
په یوه ندی	pəywəndí relation; connection (bə...əwə, ləgél: with)
په یوه ست	pəywӗst bə tied to; related to
په یوه ستی	pəywəstí bə connection with, relationship to
په ژاره	pəžarӗ sadness, sorrow
پیلان	pilán plan, scheme
پیر	pir old, aged. hatín bə ---...əwə to receive, receive hospitably

131

پیریتی	piretí oldness, antiquity
پیره میرد	pirəmérd old man; Piramerd (m.p.n.)
پیره مگرون	pirəməgrún Pira Magroon (the highest mountain in Sul. Liwa)
پیره ژن	pirežín old woman. ---əkə-i dayki his aged mother
پیروز	piróz blessed. (xwa) lə...--- bun God bless s.o. xwa le -´-bu God bless him. -´-be lə həmíwan God bless everyone. --- lə...k. to congratulate
پیروز بایی کردن له	pirozbaì k. lə to congratulate s.o.
پیروزه	pirozé topaze
پیروزی	pirozí blessing, benediction
پیرو لاوان	pirulawán young and old
پیس	pis dirty; filthy
پیش خواردن	piš: ---y xwardín to swirl (pent-up emotions)
پیشان دان	pišan d. to show s.th. -´-ïm də show it to me
پیشاندەر	pišandér compass
پیشانگا	pišaŋgá exhibit
پیشـه	pišé occupation, trade, profession; trait, quality
پیشه سازی	pišəsazí crafts; industry
پیت	pit abundance, fecundity, productivity. bə --- fertile, rich
پچکولـه	pĭčkolé (dim. of pĭčúk) little, small
پچرین	pĭčrín (pĭčr-) to cut, sever. le pĭčirrín (pass.) to give out, be at an end (strength, etc.). hezi le ʔəpĭčirre his strength gives out

132

پچوك pĭčúk = bĭčúk   small

پف pĭf   puff (of smoke)

پلـ pĭlé   rung of ladder; grade, stage, level; degree (of temp.)

پـرد pĭrd   bridge

پروژه pĭrožé   project

پرسين pĭrsín (pĭrs-)   to ask (a question) (lə: of)

پرسيار pĭrsyár   question. ---i mıllí plebiscite. --- lə...k.   to ask s.o. a question

پرشنگ pĭršĭŋ   radiation; ray, sparks (of light, anger, etc.)

پرتقال pĭrtĭqál   orange (fruit)

پرژاندن pĭržandín (pĭržen-)   to sprinkle, scatter. həwr mĭrwarí ʔəpĭržene   the clouds sprinkle pearls

پرلـ pĭř lə...(əwə)   full of. lə --- all of a sudden. --- k.   to fill s.th. up

پرمانـا pĭřmaná   meaningful

پررسـام pĭřsám   fraught with awe, awful, terrible

پررتاو pĭřtáw   running fast, full-speed

پرو پچ pĭřupúč   nonsense

پساندن pĭsandín (psen-)   to break, sever

پسمام pĭsmám   cousin

پشكنين pĭškĭnín (pĭškĭn-)   to search carefully, examine, inspect

پشكـو pĭškó   (glowing) embers

پشت pĭšt   back; support; behind. --- bə xwá with God's help. lə ---...(əwə) behind. --- gĭrdín   to support, bolster

پشتين pĭštén   belt, sash

133

پشتگیر کردن	pĭštgir: ---i...k. to support, back up s.o.
پشتگیری کردن	pĭštgirì k. to support
پشــو	pĭšú a breath; rest, pause. --- pya hatĭnəwé to sigh deeply (in satisfaction)
پتـو	pĭtéw solid, firm, strong
پتـوی	pĭtəwí solidity, compactness
پتـــر	pĭtír lə more than
پزیشك	pĭzíšk doctor, physician
پلنگ	plĭŋ tiger
پــلاو	pḻaw pilaf
پــول	pol class, grade (in school); group, flock; squadron; flight (aviation)
پولیس	polís police, policeman
پولا	poḻá steel
پوپنه	popné comb (of domestic fowl)
پور	por black partridge, francolin
پوستال	postál (heavy) shoes
پوسته	posté post office
پوش	poš (usually as suffix) clad, wearing. šinpóš wearing blue
پوشته وپه ردا خ	poštewpərdáx well-dressed, well-groomed
پروگــرام	prográm program
پرو په لانتــا	propəlantá propaganda
پشیلــه	pšilé cat
پشودان	pšudán comfortable
پوچ	puč coreless nut; empty (nut)

پو ل   pul¹ unit of money

پو ل   pul² checker, draughts

پو ل   pul³ postage stamp

پوور   pur aunt (paternal or maternal)

پوورزا   purzá aunt's son or daughter; cousin

پو ش   puš straw, hay

پیا   pya (prep., = contraction of péda) in, into, etc. ʔáheki pya yetəwə a bit of strength comes back to him. --- nán to press down on. pənjéti pyá nə press your finger down on it

پیاسه   pyasé a stroll; walk. --- k. to go for a walk

پیاو   pyaw man; husband; servant; king (cards); person, (any)one. pyáwəkə (voc.) my husband! ---əgəwrəkán dignitaries. ---anə manfully

پیاو چاك   pyawčák good man or men; sensible men

پیاوه تی   pyawətí manliness

پیاوکوشتن   pyawkuštín murder

پیاز   pyaz onions

پیاز فروش   pyazfïróš onion seller

ق   q

تا تا   qá! qá! (onom. of laughter) ha! ha!

قائد   qaʔíd general (military). ---i fırqé division commander (mil.)

تاچ   qač leg

قادر   qadír Qadir (m.p.n.)

135

تاجار	qajár Qajar (Iranian dynasty, 1796-1925)
تالــــی	qalí carpet
تالــب	qalíb mold; shape
تالـــور	qalór outside cover; shell; skin
تاپی	qapí entrance
تاپوت	qapút overcoat; game, esp. backgammon, won by getting all the tricks
تارچك	qarčík mushrooms
تاره مان	qaremán brave man, hero. ---ané heroically
تاره مانـــی	qaremaní heroism; heroic deed
تارس بوون	qars be...b. to be displeased by, to dislike. žínekéši beme --- ʔebe his wife also will find this objectionable
تاسم	qasím Qasim (m.p.n.)
تاش	qaš slice (of fruit, etc.)
تــات	qat (following a numeral) -fold
تاوه	qawé coffee
تاوه یی	qaweí brown
تایم	qayím hard, firm, strong (clothes, rope, bldg., etc.). --- qse k. to talk loudly. --- k. to strengthen; to fortify (a place)
تاییش	qayıš chain; strap. ---i seʕát watch band
تــاز	qaz goose; swan
تازانج	qazánj profit; interest. dé fılsım --- kırd I made 10 fils profit
تازه وان	qazewán goosetender
تاضی	qazí Cadi (Muslim judge)

136

قـاژ   qaž   jackdaw

قيزوبيز   qèzubéz   aversion, repugnance

قەبەر   qəbér   grave (n.). bə ---i báwkïm   by my father's grave!

قەبول كردن   qəbúl k.   to accept, receive

قـەد   qəd: see bəqéd

قەدەغە   qədəɣé   suspension; prohibition, ban. --- k.   to ban, prohibit, suspend

بە قەدەر   qədér   amount. bə ---   in proportion to; in the amount of

قەدپال   qədpál   mountain slopes

قـدرى   qədrí   Qadri (m.p.n.)

قەفەس   qəfés   cage

قـەل   qəl   crow

قەلەباچكە   qələbačké   magpie

قەلەرەشە   qələřəšé   crow

قەلا   qəlá   fort, fortress

قەلاچو   qəlačó   killing off, extermination

قەلاچوالان   qèlačwalán   Qalachwalan (place near Sul.)

قـلادزه   qəladïzé   Qaladiza (place name)

قەلەبالغى   qələbalɣí   crowd of people

قەلەبالـغ   qələbalíɣ   crowd of people

قەلەم   qələm   pencil; pen

قەلەمباز   qələmbáz   hopping; jumping, gamboling (n.)

قەلەو   qələw   fat. lam-i ---   the velarized l

قەپقەپ   qəpqép   (wooden) slippers

قەراغ   qəráɣ   edge; outlying district

ته ره هه نجیر	qerèhənjír Karahanjir (a place near Kirkuk)
ته رن	qərn century
ته ریولـــ	qəryolé bed
ته رز	qərz debt
ته رزدار	qərzdár debtor
ته شه	qəšé priest, minister
ته شه نگ	qəšéŋ beautiful; attractive
ته صــاب	qəṣáb butcher
ته تــار	qətár a kind of Kurdish song; caravan
ته تیس	qətís dammed up, confined (to a place). --- mán to be pent up, lodged in place. ---máw stuck, lodged in place
ته ومان لـــ	qəwmán (qəwme-) lə... to befall someone (disaster). wəku šteki le qəwmabe as if s.th. (terrible) had happened to him. leqəwmáw bereaved
ته وس	qəws parenthesis
ته وزه	qəwzé scum
ته ی ناكـــا	qəy: --- naka it doesn't matter; never mind. --- čí ʔəka what does it matter? what difference will it make?
ته یچی	qəyčí scissors
ته یسـه ر	qəysér Caesar; czar
ته یسی	qəysí apricot
ته زا	qəzá predestined accident. bé ---bi may you be without accident! (formula) God protect you
قیمه ت	qimét value
تینه به ری كیشان له	qinəbəri kešán (keš-) lə... to persevere in showing hostility against

قیرتــاو   qirtáw tar; asphalt

قیت   qit upright, erect. xoy --- k. to stand erect, straighten up

قیژاندان   qižandín (qišen-) to scream, yell

قیژەقیژ   qižəqíž howling, yelling (n.)

قنبلـه   qïnbïlé bomb. ---i zuřıyé atomic bomb

قنج   qïnj upright (posture); slightly turned up (nose)

قنگ   qïŋ buttocks

هەلقرچان   həḻ qïrčán to sizzle, burn. həlqïrčáw burning

ترچەقرچ   qïrčeqïrč splintering sound

ترپوك   qïrpók dried up; bad (raisins, grapes, dates)

قســه   qïsé, qse talk, talking. ---i hıčupúč nonsense. ---i pešunyán proverb. ---i xer a favorable word, a good word (in behalf of s.o.). --- dər bïrín (br-) to utter a word. --- pe bïrín to interrupt s.o. --- k. to talk. ---i tya k. to comment on, remark on. henánə qïsə kïrdïn to engage s.o. in conversation

قشلــه   qïšḻé barracks

قــژ   qïž hair (of the head)

قبلــه نما   qıblenïmá compass

قوچ   qoč ram

قــول   qoḻ arm; shirt sleeve, cuff

توناغ   qonáɣ stage, interval of time; stage in a journey

توندەره   qondəré lady's shoes

قونتەرات   qonterát contract

تو پچه	qopčé button. ---i qól cuff link
قوراوی	qorawí socks
قـورت	qórt stumbling-block; obstacle
قـــوخ	qox peach
قـــوز	qoz elegant
قـــوزی	qozí grace, elegance
قسه	qsə: see qǐsé talk
قـــوو	qu swan
تو چاندن	qučandín (quček-) to clench, make a fist; to shut (eyes) tight
قـــوول	qul deep, profound
قفل	qufl lock
هەلقولان	qulán (qule-): həl --- to gush out, well out from, surge from
تولپ دان	qulp d. to boil(water, etc.)
تومار کردن	qumarkǐrdín gambling (n.)
قرآن	qurʔán Koran
توربان	qurbán sacrifice. bə ---i...b. to be sacrificed for. dáykǐm bə ---y bet may my mother be sacrificed for her (i.e., because of her great beauty she deserves such an honor). Also used honorifically for person addressed: --- naw číyə? what is your name?
تورباننـی	qurbaní immolation, sacrifice; sacrificial victim
لـچ هەلقور چاندن	qurčandín (qurček-): lǐč --- to bite one's lips (in disapproval), to pout
قورگ	qurg throat
قورتوشم	qurqúšǐm lead (metal)

قــــورس	qʋrs heavy
قورسایی	qʋrasí weight
قـــــورر	quř mʋd
قـــــوراوی	quřawí mʋd-covered
قوتابی	qʋtabí student
قوتابخانه	qʋtabxané school. ---kan-i mamwestayán normal schools. ---i pišesazí technical school
قوتـــــو	qʋtú box
قـــــووه ت	quwét strength. be --- weak. bə --- strong
قـــوژ بن	qužbín nook, corner

ر   ř

را	řaᴵ opinion, idea, view. ləsər --- b. to be of an opinion. ləsər ʔem---yəm I am of the opinion that...
را	řaᴮ away (particle forming phrases with verbs, under which they are listed)
رابه ر	řabér quide
رابوردو	řabʋrdú previous, past, gone by
راده	řadé extent, degree; figures, statistics. ta -´-yek to a certain degree. ta čï-´-yek to what extent. ---i ʔasaí average amount
رادیو	řadyó radio
راکیشان	řakešán a drawing (in a lottery)
راکردن	řakïrdín running away, flight
راماظان	řamazán ᴿamazan

141

ران   řan¹   thigh

ران   řan²   flock (of sheep)

راپه‌ رین   řapəřín   jumping up (n.)

راسپارده   řaspardé   an errand (for s.o.). --- gəyandïn   to do an errand

راست   řast   true, right, correct; truthful, correct; honest, sincere; right, right hand side. -´-ït ʔəwe   if you want the truth, to tell the truth. --- k. to be correct, be right. řást ʔəkəy, řázəkəy you are right. --- k.əwé to rectify, correct, set right

راسته   řasté   right-handed; straight-edge, rule

راسته تینه   řastəqiné   true; genuine, real; orthodox

راسته وراست   řastəwřást   straight, directly

راسته وخو   řastəwxó   direct, directly, immediately

راست‌گویی   řastgoí   trustworthiness, fidelity

راستی   řastí   truth, reality; the best part, the good side (of s.th.). řastekéy the truth of the matter. bə -´-, lə -´-ya as a matter of fact, really. ʔəwə-i -´-be to tell the truth

راستی په رست   řastïpəříst   truth-loving person; honest

راو   řaw   hunt, hunting (n.). bïn --- the terminal point in a hunt. sər --- the beginning point in a hunt

راوه ستاو   řawəstáw   standing up (adj.), the one standing up

راوه ژیشك   řawəžišïk   hedgehog-hunting; hedgehog hunt

راوو شكار   řàwušïkár   hunting and shooting (n.)

راخراو   řaxïráw   (pass. part. of řa xïstïn) carpeted

رازانده‌ وه   řazandnəwé   embellishment, bedizenment, trimmings

رازی بون لــــ	řazi b. lə to be satisfied, content with, to agree to or on
ری	ře road, path, way. bém---yə bïřó go this way. lə ---i...əwə by means of; for. --- te čun to appear believable, reasonable. ---i...dán to allow s.o. -́--yan nə̀dabun they did not let them in. --- kəwtïn to reconciliate; to happen, occur. wá --- kəwtųwə it has so come to pass..., bə --- kəwtïn to set out, move along. bïrdnə bə ---wə to execute, carry out. kəwtnə -́-- to set off, start out. --- xïstïn to arrange, prepare for
ریباز	řebáz path
ریبەری کـردن	řebərí...k. to guide s.o.
ریــگا ، ریگە	řegá, řegé road, way; way (to do s.th.), manner; opportunity, chance for. lə---...da for the sake of, for
ریك	řek straight; direct; arranged, in order
بە ریكەوت	řekéwt chance, accident. bə --- by chance, accidentally, unintentionally
ریك و پیك	řekupék ,in order, well-arranged, orderly. --- xïstïn to formulate; to regulate
ریك و پیكـی	rèkupekí orderly arrangement
ریكخراو	řekxïráw organization
ری رە و	řeřéw a much-traveled road, a major thoroughfare; processional parade
ریستن	řestïn (řes-) to weave, spin
ریوی	řewí fox
ریــــز	řez¹ row, series
ریــــز	řez² respect; reverence. bə --- respected, respectable, honorable, esteemed; with,respect, respectfully. --- lə... gïrtïn to respect, show honor to s.o.
ریزگرتن	řezgïrtín, bəřezgïrtïn respect, high regard. Neg.: lack of respect, disrespect for

143

ریز لیگراو   řezlegráw respected

ره زیم   řežím political set-up, regime

ره چه له ك   řečelék root; stock, breed. ---i...bǐrinewé to eradicate, extirpate

ره فیق   řefíq friend; Rafiq (m.p.n.). ˤelí- -´-tan your friend Ali

رغبه ت   řeɣbét bo wish, desire

ره غنه   řeɣné criticism. --- le...gǐrtín to criticize s.o.

ره حه ت   řehét comfortable, at ease; free from trouble or annoyance

ره حم   řehm mercy, compassion. be --- merciful

ره نج   řenj hard work, drudgery, toil. --- k., --- kešán to drudge, toil, labor

ره نگ   řeŋ color. be híč ---ek in no way. -´-e, --- héye (foll. by subjunct.) perhaps. --- henánu bǐrdin to lose one's color, one's face turns pale

ره نگاو ره نگ   řeŋáwřeŋ (pleasantly) multicolored; variegated

ره نگین   řeŋín multicolored, colorful

ره ق   řeq hard; rigid

ره سام   řesám artist, painter

ره سم   řesǐm picture; portrait

ره سمگر   řesmgír photographer

ره سمی   řesmí official (adj.), having an official status

ره سمکیش   řesmkéš camera

ره ش   řeš black; dark. čarenus-i --- bad luck

ره شه با   řešebá dust storm, resheba

رشید	ř̆əšíd Rashid (m.p.n.)
ره شول	ř̆əšól Rashol (m.p.n.)
ره ش پوش	ř̆əšpóš clothed in black, wearing black (sign of mourning)
ره واج	ř̆əwáj popularity
ره وان	ř̆əwán smooth and clear, smooth flowing
ره واندز	ř̆əwandíz Rawanduz (town in Arbil Liwa)
ره واندنه وه	ř̆əwandnəwə́ (ř̆əwen-) to force apart, open up, separate
ره وانه کردن	ř̆əwanə́ k. to send, dispatch
ره وشت	ř̆əwíšt conduct, behavior
ره وت	ř̆əwt trot; graceful movement
ره خنه	ř̆əxnə́ criticism; objection. --- lə... gïrtïn to criticize s.o.
ره خنه گر	ř̆əxnəgïr critic
ره زامه ندی به رامبه ربه	ř̆əzaməndí bərambər bə favorable disposition towards, consent, agreement to
ره ز ایی	ř̆əzaí satisfaction; pleasure
ریش	ř̆iš beard. --- tašín to shave (intr.)
ریشه	ř̆išə́ rootlet
ریان	ř̆iyán (ř̆i-) to defecate
ریاضه	ř̆iyazə́ sports
ریز	ř̆iz line, row; rank. náwi yetə ---i... its name joins the ranks of...
رفاندن	ř̆ïfandín (rfen-) to grab, snatch, steal, kidnap
رنین	ř̆ïnín (ř̆m-) to pluck (fruit from a tree)
خور نینه وه	xoy ř̆ïninəwə́ (ř̆m-) to tear out ones hair, scratch o.s. (in grief or anger)

145

رق	řĭq anger, rage
دارشتن	da řĭštĭn (řež-) to cast (metal)
رزگار	řĭzgár free, safe. --- b. to be safe. --- k. to rescue, save s.o. (le dəst-i...: from the hands of)
رزگار بوون	řĭzgarbún rescue, saving (of s.o.)
رزگاری	řĭzgarí deliverance, emancipation, rescue
رجا کردن	řja lə...k. to beg of s.o. -´-tan le ʔəkəm I beg of you
روح	řoẖ spirit; soul
رولــ	řolə́ offspring, son, daughter. ---i širínĭm my dear son!
رولەرو	řoləró rolaro (lament uttered by mothers bewailing the death of their children)
رومانـــسى	řomaní Rumanian
رون	řon oil; clarified butter; lard
روشن کردن	řošĭn k. to light up, illuminate s.th. for...
روشن بیر	řošĭnbír enlightened
روشنایی	řošnaí glimmer, light, illumination. ləbər ---i- under the aegis of
رویشتن	řoyštĭn (řo-) to go, go away (cf. čun to go [to a place]). ləsər...---, --- ləsər to go on, continue (doing s.th.); to follow, adopt (a course of action)
رویشتەوه	řoyštnəwé (řó-) to go back, return
روژ	řož sun; day. -´- baš good morning! ʔəw---ə́ on that day, at that time. ---əkéy on that day. -´-ek le ---án one day, once. ləm---anéda in the past few days. ---i čwàr-i máŋ on the fourth of the month. ---i dwaí on the next day. ---i řəš an ill-fated day. ---an-i məktéb school days. dwa --- future. ---anə daily

146

روژئاوا	řòž∂awá, řozawá west
روژباش لی کردن	řožbáš le k. to greet s.o.
روژ هەلات	řožhəlat, řožəlát east. ---i nawřást The Mɪ̄ddle East
روژگار	řožgár all day long
روژ نامه	řožnamə́ newspaper. ---i žɪ́n the news- paper "Zhin"
روژ نامه چی	řožnaməčɪ́ newspaperman
روژوو	řožú fasting (n.). bə --- fasting (adj.)
روو	řu face; facet; front. --- bə --- face to face; bluntly, frankly. bərəw --- in front of; in the face of. lə́m---∂wə on this subject. lə yə́k ---∂wə on one side. bə ---i...da in the direction of. lə ---i...(əwə) with respect to, in reference to. --- d. to occur, take place. ---y həbún to be so bold as to; neg.: to be shy, bashful. ---t nɪ́yə you are shy. --- k.ə to go toward; to turn to, face s.o. ---y kɪ̈rdə mɪn he turned to me. ---...te k. to turn around, turn and look at s.o.; to visit, frequent (a place). -́--yan tè ʔəkat he turns and looks at them. xɪ̈stnə --- to uncover, expose; to express (opinion, etc.). ʔə́mpɪ̄rsyarè ʔəxəynə --- we pose this question
رو بار	řubár river
رودا و	řudáw event; happening
روود راو	řudɪ̈ráw event
روو که ش	řukə́š coating, overlay
روون کردنه وه	řun k.əwə́ to clarify, explain. With kə: to make it clear, demonstrate that...
رو ناك	řunák illuminating, shining, bright
روناكـــی	řunakɪ́ light, illumination
روون کردنه وه	řunkɪ̈rdnəwə́ elucidation, clarification

147

روو شکین کردن	řušĭken k. to shame, put to shame
روت	řut bare, naked. --- k. to undress. --- k.əwə to rob, plunder (highwayman)
روتــی	řutí nakedness
رواین	řuwanín (řwan-) to look
رووەو	řuwéw towards, in the direction of
روخان	řuxán (řuxe-) to collapse (intr.)
روخاندن	řuxandín¹ (ruxen-) to demolish
روخاندن	řuxandín² demolition, destruction
روخــاو	řuxáw having collapsed, collapsed
روســی	řusí Russian
روخســار	řuxsár face, visage
روالـــت	řwaḻét appearance
روان	řwan (řwe-) to grow (intr.) ʔéw darè báš řwawə that tree has grown up well
رواندن	řwandín (řwen-) to grow s.th.
رواینن	řwanín (řwan-) to glance over, survey

س s

ســا...یـــا	sa...ya (foll. by subjunct.) whether...or
سابون	sabún soap
ســاده	sadé plain (color)
ساغ	saɣ, sax safe. --- b.əwə to become crystal clear
ساغوسـەلیم	saɣusəlím safe and sound
ساحه	sahé yard, ground. ---i fudbóḻ football field
ساکار	sakár simple

ساكارى	sakarí simplicity. bə --- superficially
ســـال	saḻ see s̲aḻ year
سام	sam fear, awe. --- lə...ništín terror settles on...
سامان	samán wealth. ---əkan-i naw?érz mineral riches
سامدار	samdár awe-inspiring; frightening, terrifying
هەلســان	san (s-): həḻ --- to wake up; to stand up. bə...həḻ --- to perform (a task), satisfy (a need). bə̀m pewistə̀ həḻ nás̲e it does not meet this requirement
هەلساندن	sandín (sen-): həḻ --- to cause to stand, arouse
ساندنەوه	sandínəwə́ (sen-) to obtain, get
سانەوى ، ثانوى	sanəwí secondary
ســارد	sard cold; numb. --- k.əwə́ lə... to make s.o. cold to... ?əmə mamostakán --- ?əkatəwə lə ?íš̲yan this will make the teachers lose interest in their work
ساردا	sardá cold (n.). ---y b. to be cold. --́-mə I'm cold. ---t nî́yə aren't you cold?
سارغى	sarɣí bandage
ساروخ	sarúx rocket
ساسانى	sasaní Sassanian
سات	sat time. ?ə́w---ə̀ at that time
سارا	sawá infant, child
ساون	sawǔn whetting, honing (usually on piece of stone)
ساختمان	saxtĭmán construction, building

149

سبه ینی	sbéyne tomorrow
سی	se three. --- bə --- three by three. ---yanəkè-i tíryan the other three men
سیه ر	sebér shadow; shade
سیه ردار	sebərdár shady
سیداره	sedaré gallows
سی هه مین	sehəmín = seyém third
سیمساله	sesalé three-year-old (goat, sheep)
سی شه مه	sešəmmé Tuesday
سیو	sew apples. ---i bĭn ʔərz potato
سیودوو	sèwdú hesitation, vacillation. be --- without hesitation. lə...da --- k. to be at sixes and sevens, hesitate, vacillate over
سیه م	seyém third
سید	seyíd, səy Sayyid (title given to descendents of Muhammad through his daughter Fatima)
سه طت	seʕát hour; watch; clock. --- šéš-i ʔewarè 6:00 p.m.
سه عی	seʕí studying, schoolwork; homework. --- k. to study (hard)
سه باره ت به	səbarét bə with regard to, with respect to, as to
سه به ت	səbəté basket
سه د	səd, sədé: see ṣəd, ṣədé
سه د ه ف	sədéf mother of pearl
سه گ	səg dog
سه هل	séhĭl easy
سه هول	səhól ice

150

سه‌کـو   səkú   platform; mound

سـلام   səlám   peace. ---u ʕəléyk greetings!
--- le k. to send s.o. one's regards.
brakém ---ĭt le ʔəka my brother şends
you his regards. --- bə...gəyandĭn to
give s.o.'s regards to... ---i mĭni pe
bĭgəyénə give him my regards

سلامـت   səlamét   safety. -́- bi thank you (said
in response to certain expressions)

سه‌ما کردن   səma k.   to dance

سه‌ماوه‌ر   səmawér   samovar

سه‌مه‌ره   səmərə́   events, incidents

سمین   səmín   cavity

سه‌مون   səmmún   bread rolls

سه‌ندن   səndĭn (sənd-)   to take, acquire; to receive

سه‌ندنه‌وه   səndĭnəwə́ (sənd-)   to receive, accept

سه‌نگـر   səŋér, səŋŋér   barricade, entrenchment;
bulwark, rempart

سه‌پاندن (به‌سه‌ر)   səpandĭn (səpen-): bəsər...--- to impose,
force on

سـر   sər   head; hair; top, crest; aspect, side.
lə ---ek-i tĭrišəwə on the other hand. lə
-́-əwə above. --- bə subordinate to;
dependent on. ---.lə from the beginning
of. --- lə bəyaní the first thing in the
morning. ---, lə --- on, on top of; about
bə ---ya over it. (wəxt) bə --- bĭrdĭn to
while away, spend (time). --- bĭřĭn to
kill, slaughter. --- le dər čún to understand, comprehend. -́-ĭm le dər náče I
don't understand. bo...čunə --- to pass
without difficulty for... bóman náčetə ---
we will not achieve it with impunity. ---
lə...d, ---i...d. to visit, pay a visit
to. ، --- da henán to comb one's hair. ---
kəwtĭn to succeed; to win (bəsər: over).

--- lə...da k. to take one's mind off of.
min ---i le da nákəm I can't take my mind
off of it. --- da nəwandïn (nəwen-) to
bow one's head down to s.o. (in submission);
to make s.o. bend the head down (in submission). --- lə...həl pečán (peč-) tọ be
at variance with, contradict. --- xïstïn
to raise up, elevate

سه را	sərá palace; government office bldg.
سه ربان	sərbán roof
سه رباز	sərbáz soldier
سه ربه	sərbé allied with; under the guidance of
سه ربه ست	sərbést free, independent; free (lə: to)
سه ربه ستى	sərbəstí freedom
سه ربه خو	sərbəxó independent
سه ربه خوى	sèrbəxoí independence
سه رچاوه	sèrčawé fountainhead; source (esp. scien- tific), reference work
سه رچنار	sèrčïnár (place near Sul.)
سه ردان	sərdán a visit (lə: to)
سه ردار	sərdár military general (high-ranking military personnel)
سه رده م	sərdém age, period
سه ردل	sərdïl heart
سه ره	səré period; era, time
سه ره ك	sərék leader. --- jəmhʊryət president (of a republic). --- wəzirán prime minister
سه ره كى	sərekí main, principal
سه ره رای	sérəra-i in addition to. ---i ʔəwə furthermore

سه‌ره‌ت	**sərətá** beginning (n.); title, heading (of article, etc.). ---i maŋekə-i tïr the beginning of next month
سه‌ره‌تیی	**sərətaí** primitive, beginning (adj.); elementary. məktəb-i --- elementary school
سه‌ره‌تان	**sərətán** cancer
سه‌ره‌وه	**sérəwə** above, up; upstairs. lə -́-yə it is upstairs
سه‌رف کردن	**sərf k.** to spend (money)
سه‌رگه‌ردانی	**sərgərdaní** misfortune, calamity
سه‌رگوزه‌شته	**sərguzəšté** story, tale; anecdote
سه‌رین	**sərín** pillow
سه‌رنج	**sərínj** scrutiny; suggestion. --- lə...d. to examine carefully. --- řa kešán to draw the attention of s.o. ---i řá kešam it attracted my attention
سه‌رکه‌وتن	**sərkəwtín** success
سه‌رکه‌وتو	**sərkəwtú** victorious; victor
سه‌رکرده	**sərkïrdé** leader, chief. --- k. to lead, guide through
سه‌رکرده‌یی	**sərkïrdəí** leadership. bə ---i under the leadership of
سه‌رما	**sərmá** cold (n.), coldness. ʔém---yè čénd dəwam ʔəka? how long will this cold last? ---y bún to be cold. -́-yeti he is cold. -́-man níyə we are not cold
سه‌روک	**sərók** leader; chief
سه‌روکایه‌تی	**sərokayətí** leadership
سه‌رپاك	**sərpák** all, entire
سه‌رسام بوون	**sərsam b.** to be dismayed, confused; to be kept in suspense. --- k. to astonish. --- mán to be puzzled, amazed (kə...čon...? at how...)

153

سەرسەخت	sərséxt stubborn; refractory; unyielding
سەرسوچ	sərsúč corner, angle. ---i kolán a bend in the road; street corner
سەرشاخ	səršáx mountaintop
سەرشەقام	səršəqám Sarshaqam (quarter in Sul.)
سەرو	séru cypress
سەروماڵ	sərumál all that is dear or valuable, all of one's possessions
سەرومل	sərumíl head and neck; the part of the body including thorax and head
سەرومر	sərumír entirely; all together
سەروپی	sərupé a dish made of the head and feet of sheep or goats
سەروخوار	səruxwár top and bottom; north and south
سەروەستا	sərwəstá master craftsman; foreman
سەریشی	səryešé headache
سەرژمیری	səržmerí head-count; census
سەتـل	sétïl bucket
سەوا	səwá haggling. --- k. to haggle, bargain
سەوز	səwz: see sₑwz green
سەخت	səxt difficult, hard; rigorous; rugged; inaccessible; strong; invincible
سەی	səy = səyíd Sayyid (title given to descendents of Muhammad through his daughter Fatima)
سەیر	səyr¹ strange, odd
سەیر	səyr² sight, view. ---i k. to look at, watch, see; to consider, study, observe
سەیران	səyrán picnic, outing

سەیران که ر   səyrankér picnicker

سەیرکه ر   səyrkér spectator, on-looker

سەیوان   səywán Saywan (a hill very close to Sul.; it is the site of the main cemetery of the city)

سى   si thirty. ---w yék 31

سیفون   sifón soda pop

سینه ما   sinəmá cinema; movies

سییره   siré hiss, hissing (n.)

سیروان   sirwán the Sirwan River

سیسارك   sisárk bald vulture

سیخور   sixór porcupine

سك   sïk, sïg belly, stomach; womb. ---y čun to have diarrhoea. -́-ïm ʔəče I have diarrhoea

سکرتیر   sïkïrtér secretary

سلیمان   sïlemán Sulaiman (m.p.n.)

سلاو کردن لــ   sïl̲aw lə...k. to say "səlamuʕələyk" to, greet s.o.

سلق   sïl̲q garden beet

سمت   sïmt buttock

سنور   sïnúr boundary, bound; limit. be --- unlimited. --- bə...d. to delimit, define

سنوربیدان   sïnurpedán defining, delimiting (n.)

سیی   sïpí white. --- k. to whiten

سپلەیی   sïpl̲əí ungratefullness, ingratitude

سپیاو   sïpyáw white face powder. --- k. to cover the face with sipyaw, to powder one's face

سرینه وه	sïrinəwə́ (sr-) to erase, expunge
سرپه سرپ	sïrpəsïrp k. to whisper
سرود	sïrúd anthem, patriotic song
سروشت	sïrúšt nature
ستهم	sïtə́m hard, difficult
سزا	sïza¹ agony; torture. --- d. to pain, torture s.o.
سزا	sïzá² Siza (m.p.n.)
سفره	sɪfrə́ tablecloth
سفتاح	sɪftáh̲ first sale (of the day, of a new business, etc.). --- k. to have one's inaugural sale. ʔəmřo -´-ïm nə́kïrduwə I haven't sold anything yet today
سحر	sïh̲ïr magic
سحربازی	sɪh̲ïrbazí sorcery
سنف	sínïf class (in school, etc.)
سیاده ت	sɪyadə́t Excellency (title of respect given to high-ranking officials)
صیانه	sɪyanə́ maintenance
سیاسی	sɪyasí political; politics
سکوت	skut silence. --- k. to be, remain silent; to refuse to talk
	sl- see sïl-
سنوق	snoq, snuq box
صوفی	sofí Sufi
سوران	során Soran (the southern part of Kurdistan)
سورانی	soraní Sorani
سوفیه ت	sovyə́t Soviet

سپاردن   spardín (sper-) to entrust, commit (bə: to) bə xwát ʔəsperɪm I entrust you to God. řa --- to order, command

سپاس   spas, sʊpás thanks. ---i...k. to thank. ʔəməwe ---i nusér bkəm I want to thank the author. ---ɪt ʔəkəm thank you

هەلستان   stan (ste-): həl --- = həl sán to arise; to stand up. bə...həl --- to perform (mission, task, etc.). ʔáya ʔədəb-i kʊrdí bə dəwr-i xoy hél ʔəse does Kurdish literature play its role?

سووچ   súč corner

سوچدار   sučdár angular, sharp-cornered

سود   sud benefit, interest, advantage. bə --- useful, advantageous. --- lə...wər gɪ̈rtɪn to derive benefit from

سودی   sudí effectiveness

سووك   suk light (weight)

سومەری   sumərí Sumerian

سوور   sur red. --- həlgəráw reddened, reddish. --- k.əwé to fry

هەل سوراندن   surandín (suren-): həl --- to carry out, perform; to wield

سوورانەوه   suranəwé (sure-) to walk idly, loiter about

سوراو   suráw rouge (cosmetics)

سوور بوون بو   surbún bo determination, resolve to (do s.th.)

سوورەوه کردن   surəwə k. to bake

سووری   surí Syrian

سووتان   sután[1] (sute-) to burn

سوتان   sután² burning; conflagration

سوئال   suʔál question

سوجاد   sujád rug, inferior kind of carpet made of wool yarn

سوكان   sukán steering wheel

سليمانى   suleymaní, slemaní Sulaimania

سلطه   sulté power, authority

سونى   sunní Sunni

سوپا   supá, spa army

سوپاس   supás = spas thanks

سوار   swar rider, horseman. ---i...b. to mount, ride. ---i...k. to mount, ride s.o. on... šallá --- -i kérekišyan bïkïrditayə I wish they had also ridden you around on a donkey

سواره   swaré equestrian, horseman, rider

سويد   swíd Sweden

سيانزه   syanzé thirteen

ش š

شا   ša king, monarch, shah; the largest of a species. nadïr ---i həwšár Shah Nadir Afshar

شادهمار   šadəmár the largest blood vessel; the vital vein or nerve

شادمانى   šadïmaní happiness

شاهنشا   šahənšá king of kings; the Shah (of Iran)

شاهنشاهى   šàhənšahí imperial (of Iran)

شایی	šaí ceremony; festivity, celebration
شاللا	šálla (foll. by subjunct.) God willing; I hope
شاملوو	šamló, šamlú Shamlo (place name)
شان	šan shoulder
شانازی کردن	šanazi k. bǝ... to be proud of. --́-- ǝkǝn bǝwǝ kǝ kúrdǐn they are proud to be Kurds
شانه	šané comb
شانزه	šanzé sixteen
شار	šar city, town. lǝ ---i nуʋyórk in the city of New York
شارباژیر	šarbažér Sharbazher (place name)
شاردنه وه	šardnǝwé (šar-) to conceal, hide
شاره وانی	šarǝwaní municipality
شاره ویران	šarǝwerán destroyed cities, cities in ruins
شازه زا	lǝ...šarǝzá familiar with; well-versed on; expert on
شاره زوور	šarǝzúr Sharazur (plain near Sul.)
شاری	šarí city-dweller, city-folk; city-bred
شارستانیه تی	šarǐstanetí civilization; city life
شارودی	šárudé downs and villages
شاتوو	šatú blackberry
شاخ	šax mountain. ---i goyža Mt. Goyzha (N.E. of Sul.)
هه لشاخان	šaxán (šaxe-): hǝl̲ --- to reprimand, rebuke, berate
شاخودان	šăxudáx mountains

159

شايانى	šayàn-i worthy of, deserving
شازاده	šazadé prince; princess
شاژن	šažín queen; empress
شيلين	šelín (šel-) to be lame
شينهيى	šenəí gentleness. bə --- leisurely, slowly
شير	šer lion
شيرپهنجه	šerpənjé cancer
شيت	šet mad, maniac
شيتخانه	šetxané insane asylum
شيوه	šewé appearance, semblance; aspect, form, pattern; manner, way; dialect. bə ---yek-i mikanikí mechanically. bə ---yek-i wəxtí temporarily. bə ---yek-i wá kə in such a way that...
شيخ	šex Sheikh (title placed before names of religious men; may be inherited)
شبح	šəbéẖ ghost, apparition, spectre
شهبهق	šə́bəq dawn. --- d. to dawn; dawn approaches
شهقهدار	šəfqədár wearing a hat; having a shade (lamp, etc.)
شههين	šəhín falcon
شهكاندن	šəkandín (šəken-) to shake (trans.)
شهكاندنهوه	šəkàndnəwé (šəken-) to shake, flutter (intr.)
شهل	šəl lame, limping, crippled
بهشهلهشهل	bə šələšél lamely, with a limp
شهمال	šəmál wind

شه‌كــر   šəkír sugar

شه‌مه‌ندوفور   šəmən[d]əfér train

شه‌مه   šəmmé Saturday; day of the week. ʔəmř̌o čənd -´-yə what day (of the week) is it today?

شه‌مشه‌مه‌كويره   šəmšəməkweré bat (animal)

شه‌پول   šəpól wave

شه‌ق   šəq kick, kicking. bə yək --- with a kick. --- lə...həḻ d. to kick s.th. aside

شه‌قام   šəqám street

شه‌قــلاوه   šəqlawé Shaqlawa (a town and summer resort in Arbil Liwa)

شه‌رعى   šərʕí religious (as opp. to civil: law, etc.)

شه‌رابــى   šərabí wine-colored, bright red

شه‌ربه   šərbé water jar

شه‌ره‌ف   šəréf honor. bə --- by my honor!

شه‌رم   šərm shame; modesty. ---...gĭrtĭn to be overcome by shame. -´- gĭrtmi I was embarrassed

شه‌رت   šərt (pl.: šĭrút) condition, proviso. -´-ə (foll. by subjunct.) provided that, on condition that. -´-ə ləbéri kəy on condition that you wear it. -´-be I promise... (formula)

شه‌رر   šəř̌¹ evil

شه‌رر   šəř̌² fighting; fight, battle. --- lə bətalí čaktĭrə better fight than be idle (prov.). --- k. to fight, combat

شه‌رره‌قسه   šəř̌əqĭsé squabble, exchange of curses

شه‌ش   šəš six

شه شه م	šəšóm	sixth
شه صت	šəṣt	sixty
شه ترنج	šətrínj	chess
شــو	šəw	night; evening. --́- baš good evening! ---i řaburdú the night before. šəwé tonight
شه واره	šəwaré	night hunting
شه و چرا	šəwčĭrá	night light; lamp
شه وگار	šəwgár	all night long
شه ونم	šəwním	dew
شه وق	šəwq¹	sunlight
شــوق	šəwq²	longing, desire
شيم پوش	šimpóš	wearing blue; feeling "blue", sad
شــين	šín	blue
شـــير	šir¹	milk
شـــير	šir²	sword
شـيره خور	širəxór	infant, baby
شـيرين	širín	sweet; lovely. ---i bə...da čun to be fascinated by. ---i peya ču he was quite taken by it
شـيريني	širiní	sweets, candies
شـيروان	širwán	Shirwan (m.p.n.)
شـــيو	šíw	evening meal; supper
شيان	šiyán (še-)	to be permissible, be allowed
شفقه	šĭfqé	cap, hat
شكانـدن	šĭkandín (šken-)	to break; to disparage; to disgrace
شـكار	šĭkár	hunting, shooting

162

شكستی خواردن	šĭkĭsti xwardín to be defeated, routed
شـــل	šĭl tired, weary
شلــەژاندن	šĭləžandín (šl̩əže-) to be embarrassed, be muddled
شلپە	šĭl̩pé splash. --- hatín lə...da to be teeming, chock-full of
شمشــال	šĭmšál musical pipe, made of either metal or woōd; flute
شــریخە	šĭrixé peal, resounding (sound)
شـــروط	šĭrót, šĭrút (pl. of šərt) conditions, preconditions, circumstances
شـــرووڕ	šĭřuwíř tattered
شــت	šĭt thing. ---ek a little bit of. ---i báše that's good
شخاتــە	šĭxaté matches
شـــعر	šírĭr poetry
شـــكور	škur thanks (to God). čóni? čáki --- how are you — well, I hope?
شـــور كـــردن	šor k. to bend, lower. sər bə...---k. to bow one's head to, bow down to
شــورەت	šorét fame, good reputation
شــورش	šorĭš revolution
شــورش گیرر	šorĭšgeř revolutionary
شــوخ	šox elegant, graceful
شـــوخی	šoxí elegance; beauty
شـــو	šu husband. --- k. to get married (to a man)
شــوم	šum evil omen, bad sign
شنــاس	šunás knowing, acquainted with... zubán --- one who knows the language

163

شـووره	šuré fence, encircling wall
شـووره یی	šureí shame, disgrace
شـوشه	šušé glass
شـوشه فروش	šušefīróš glassman, glazier
شـوتی	šutí watermelon
شوباﺕ	šubát February
شوکـرانه	šukrané thanksgiving. ---i...k. to offer thanks to
شوشتن	šuštin, stin (šo-) to wash
شـوان	šwan shepherd
شـوین	šwen place; province. ---ə gištekán the public places. lə ---...da in place of. ---...kəwtin to pursue, chase after; to follow (leaders, etc.)
شـوینه وار	šwenəwár ruins
شـوین قایم کردن	šwenqayïmkïrdín fortified area, fortification

ص ṣ

به ساغـوسه لیمی	ṣaɣ = ṣaɣ: bə ṣàɣusəlimí safely
سـال	ṣal year. ṣər-i ---ٍ the beginning of the year. ---ek-i tïr next year. čənd ---ékə for some years (now). bə ---a ču old, aged. ---án ---ə for years and years. dwa --- the last year (of...). ---ané yearly, annual
صالــح	ṣalïh Salih (m.p.n.)
سـه د	ṣəd one hundred. ---u bist 120. ---əhá (foll. by sing. n.) thousands of. ---əhá həzàr hundreds of thousands
سـه ده	ṣədé century. lém --- bistəminèda in

this Twentieth Century

سه ده ها   sədəhá (pl. of sⱥd; foll. by sing. n.) hundreds of

سه گ   sⱥg, sⱥg dog

صلاح الدين   sⱥlahⱥddín Saladin

سه وز   sⱥwz green

صه وزه   sⱥwzə́ (pl. sⱥwzⱥwát) vegetables. --- gyá green grass

سنگ   sïŋ[1] chest

سنگ   sïŋ[2] peg; stake, pole

سوالت   sⱥwalə́t pottery, bowls of clay

ت   t

تا   ta[1] fever. -´-šïm hⱥbu I also had a fever

تا   ta[2] up to, as far as, until, to (prep.). --- kéy until when? --- bⱥyaní until morning. lⱥ nyʊyórkⱥwⱥ --- bⱥɣá from N.Y. to Baghdad. Foll. by indic.: until, by the time that, as long as. ta yet until he comes; by the time he comes. Foll. by subjunct.: in order that. --- bzanin in order for us to know. Foll. by neg. subjunct.: until, before. --- néynⱥwⱥ nabe bř̌oyt you mustn't leave before we get back. See also táku

تاف   taf prime; height

تاج   taj crown

تاك   tak one, single

تاكو   táku (foll. by subjunct.) so that, in order to. cf. ta

تاكوترا   takutərá several individual ones, scat-

tered along time and space; some; a few.
---yan some of them; one here and one
there

تــال   ta**l** bitter

به تــام   tam taste. bə --- delicious. --- k.
to taste s.th.

تــاپـر   tapó ghost, apparition, spectre

تــاق   taq¹ recess, niche in wall

به تاقی تـه نیا   taq²: bə --́-i tənyà alone, all by oneself

تاقـه   taqé only one, a single one. --- kúřekǐm
həyə I have only one son

تاقـه ت   taqét energy. be --́- sluggish. bə ---
patient. be --́-i you are sluggish

تاقـم   taqím group; set

تــار   tar a quitar-like instrument

تاریك   tarík dark (n.). --- da hatín darkness
falls, to get dark

تاریکی   tarikí darkness

تــاس   tas dizziness. lə --- čənəwé lə...da
to swoon, faint from...

تــاش   táš (large) stone

تاشـین   tašín (taš-) to shave (trans.); to carve.
řiš --- to shave (intr.). da --- to fit
s.th. (into s.th.) by carving. hə**l** ---
to cut out, carve out

تاسلوجه   ta**s**lujé Tasluja (place near Sul.)

لـه تــاو   taw: lə --- for fear of; because of, for
the sake of

تــاوان   tawán crime; offense. bə ---i under the
accusation of, accused of...

تــاوان بار   tawanbár wrong-doer; criminal

تاییه تی	taybətí personal, private; special, particular. řa-i ---- xóm my own personal opinion. bə --- in particular, especially
تازه	tazé new; fresh; newly, recently, just
تــی	te in, etc. (preverbal particle, used with verbs to form verbal phrases; meaning varies acc. to the phrase). See also téda, tek, tya
تــیدا	téda in. čí tedayə what is it for?
تی به ر بوون	tebər b. to attack s.th. with the idea of destroying it
تــی که ییشتوو	tegəyštú understanding person; intelligent
تــی هه لدان	tehəldán a beating
تــیك	tek together (te + yək; a preverbal particle occurring with verbs to form verbal phrases, which are listed under the verb)
تیکه ل	tekél bə mixed with
تی که لاو	tekəláw mixed together
تیکه لاوی	tekəlawí mixture. bə --- all mixed together
تی کو شان	tekošán strife, struggle
تی کو شه ر	tekošér striver; militant person, contender
تیکــرا	tékra (follows word modified) all, without discrimination or exception
تــیل	tel trap
تی په رر بون	tepərbún-i...bəsər...da elapse, passage (of time) after...
تــیر	ter satisfied, not hungry. --- lə...həl d. to have one's fill of, be tired of. --- lə...xwardin to eat one's fill of
تیرخه و بوون	terxəw b. to get enough sleep

تـأريخ	təʔríx	history
تعلــيق	teʕlíq	comment, commentary
تعــمير	təʕmír	construction, building (for human habitation)
تعــريف	təʕríf	definition
تعتــيل	təʕtíl	vacation
تە باشــير	təbašír	chalk
تە بە ق	təbéq	tray
طبقه	təbəqé	storey; level
طبيعت	təbiʕét	nature
تە بيعى	təbiʕí	natural
تـدريب	tədríb	drill; exercise (physical)
تە فروتونا كردن	téfrutunà k.	to break up (a group); to disperse, scatter (people)
تحقيق	təhqíq	investigation; questioning. --- k. to investigate
تە كــيه	təkiyé	monastery
تە ل	təl	wire. be --- wireless, radio
تە لــبه	tələbé	student
تە لــفـون	tələfón	telephone
تەلاق كە وتن	təlaq kəwtín	to be divorced
تە لــكه	tələké	treachery, deceit
تـم	təm	haze, mist, fog
تە ماعتى كردن	təmaʕ te k.	to take advantage of, exploit s.o.
تە ماشــا كردن	təmašá: ---i...k.	to look at...
تە ماتــه	təmaté	tomatoes

168

ته مه ن	təmén age (of a person). to lə čítemének-dayt? how old are you? lə ---i hə́wt salànda at the age of seven
ته مه ل	təmmál lazy. --- k. to be too lazy (to do s.th.). -́-ĭt kĭrd né̇hati you were too lazy to come
ته مسـوز	təmmíz July. čwardə-i --- the 14th of July
ته مرين	təmrín practice
ته مسيل کردن	təmsíl k. to represent
ته نانـت	tənanét even; to the extent that; so much so that
ته نه که	tənəké tin can (usually an empty five-gallon gasoline can)
ته نهـا	tənhá = tənyá only. bə --- alone
ته نشت	təníšt side; near, beside. bə, lə --- at the side of, beside
ته نـك	təńĭk thin
ته نيا	tənyá = tənhá only; alone
ته نگ	təŋ narrow; tight. bə ---...əwə b. to be concerned with..., take care of. ---i bə...həḻ čĭnín (čn-) to molest, attack, corner ... bə ---...əwə hatĭn to take pains with, take care of...
ته نگـی	təŋí tightness, narrowness; restriction (of space)
ته نگوچه لـه مه	tə̀ŋučələmé difficulty, arduous situation
تـه ب	təp a group of hills
ته په ل	təpéḻ drum
ته پولکه	təpoḻké low hill, tepe
ته قانـد ن	təqandín explosion
تقديـر	təqdír esteem; appreciation

169

تــه قــــ	təqə́ crack (of a bullet); any loud noise made by metal
تــه قــه لا	təqəlá endeavor. --- d. to struggle, endeavor for
تــه قــه تــه ق	təqətə́q beating, pounding (n.); noise of pounding (onom.)
تــه قينــه وه	təqinəwə́ (təq-) to erupt, blast; to ignite (intr.), fire
تــه قــو هوری دانـه وه	təqohoře d.əwə́ to make a racket, a great deal of noise
تــه راتين پی کردن	təraten pe k. to toss back and forth in; to bandy through; to beat s.o. up
تــه ریَقـــــی	təriqí great embarrassment, shame
تــه رخان کـرد ن (بو)	tərxán k. to devote, set aside, allot, appropriate (bo: for)
تـــه رزه	tərzə́ hail
تـــه رر	təř damp; wet
تـــه سك	təsĭk narrow, thin, small
تشکـــر	təšəkkúr thanks. --- k. to thank
تـه شریف هینان	təšrif henán (hen-) to come (honorific)
تشریح	təšrí̱h autopsy
تـه تبیقـــی	tətbiqí practical, applied, implemental
تـــــو	təw thread
تـه واو	təwáw complete; finished, ended. --- b. to be finished, come to an end. --- k. to finish, complete s.th.
به تـه واوی	təwawí: bə --- completely, entirely, exactly
تـــه ور	tə́wĭr hatchet
تـــه ورداس	təwĭrdás hoe

تــــوژم   təwížm   precipitate haste, rashness, temerity

تەوقـــی ســـر   təwq-i sér   top of the head

تەوس   téws   derision, scorn, sarcasm

تەخت   təxt   throne

تەختە   təxté   board; blackboard

تــیارە   təyaré   airplane

تەزین   təzín   numb

تفەنگ   tfəŋ = tïféŋ   rifle

تیغ   tíɣ   dagger

تیجارەتی   tijarətí   business, commerce

تیــلایـی   tilaí   looking askance. bə ---- čaw from the corner of the eye, askance

تـیمار کـردن   timar-i...k.   to treat, cure (an ill)

بە تـین   bə tín   strong

تینومه   tinú   thirst. ---y b. to be thirsty. tinúmə I am thirsty. tinúyeti he is thirsty

تیپ   tip   team; group

تـــیر   tir   arrow

تیشــک   tišk   ray. ---i róntki x-rays. ---i xór the sun's rays, sunlight

تــیژ   tiž   sharp (knife, etc.)

تفنــگ   tïféŋ   rifle. --- nán (ne-) bə...əwə to shoot...with a rifle

تــر   tïr   other, another. járek-i --- once more; next time

تــری   tïré   grapes

تریقانــەوه   tïriqanəwé (triqe-)   to guffaw

171

تــرس	tïrs fear (of). ---i baránman nə́bu ᵂe weren't afraid of rain. --- lə...ništïn fear settles on...
تر ســان	lə...tïrsán (tïrs-) to be afraid of, fear...
تـرسولــرز	tïrsulə́rz great fear, alarm
تــروكانن	tïrukandïn (truke-) to wink, blink (an eye)
تروســكه	tïruskə́ glimmer, glint
تشـریـن	tïšrín: --- ʔəwwél, ---i yəkém October. ---i duwém, --- saní November
تــكا	tka request, entreaty. --- lə...k. to beg of, entreat. --- ʔəkəm please
تــو	to¹ seed(s)
تــو	to² you (sing.)
تــوبه	tobé repentence
توكه سازی	tokməsazí toolsmithery
تــوپ	top ball; cannon. gullə --- cannon ball
تــوپین	topín (top-) to die (animal)
تــوزی	tóze(k) a little bit of; somewhat
تــوزی	trozí wild cucumber
ترو میـل	trumpél automobile
تــور	tu¹ (in oaths) by, for the sake of. --- sər-i xot by your head! I beg of you! --- xwa, txwa by God! for Heaven's sake!
تــور	tu² mulberry
تــوك	tuk hair (human)
تــوور	tur radish
تــووره بون	tuřə b. to become angry, lose one's temper

تسووش بوون   tuš: ---i...b. to meet, come across by chance; to contract (sickness). lə řega ---i ʔəhmédbum I met Ahmad on the way. ---i səřyešébu he got a headache

تسووتن   tʊtĭ́n tobacco

تسووند   tŭ́nd strong

تسووخن که وتن   tʊxĭn kəwtĭ́n to come close to; to have something to do with

تسوانا   twaná ability, capability, power. bə pe-i --- as much as possible. lə -´-y dayə it is in one's power to... lə -´- manayə it is in our power to...

تسوانەوه   twanəwé (twe-) to melt (intr.)

تسوانین   twanĭ́n (twan-) (foll. by subjunct.) to be able to..., can. ʔəttwanĭ́m I can master you. Pass.: to be possible. nátwaɲre bə bĭ́č jorek it is in no way possible

تسوانج   twánj intimation, hint

تسوی   twé slice; ply

تسیا   tya (=teda) in it. žĭn-i jwan-i tyáyə there are beautiful women in it

و ، وو   u

u, ʊ: See ʔu, ʔʊ

ف   v

ڤالسی بول   valiból volley-ball

ڤنگه ڤنگ   vĭŋəvĭ́ŋ buzzing (of a bee)

ڤره ڤر   vĭřəvĭ́ř whirring (of a machine), howling (of wind) etc.

173

و   w

و١   wa thus, so. Unstressed: already, now.
wá ʔəxom I eat like this. wa ʔəxóm I'm
eating now. --́- dyaʏə it appears, it
seems. šĭtek-i wà níyə there is no such
thing. šĭtek-i wám bist I've heard s.th.
like that. wá bzaním as far as I know.
wán lə ʕiráqda they are now in Iraq. wát
ʔəzani you would have thought... kə --́-bu
as this is the case, thus, so. cf. wók(u)

واجب   wajíb duty, obligation

والسى   walí vali, governor of an Ottoman province

واق وورمان   waq: ---y wuř mán (men-) to be greatly be-
wildered. ---y wúř ʔəmène he becomes
very puzzled

واتعى   waqıʕí actual, real

هەلواسين   wasín (was-): həḻ --- to hang s.th. up

بەواسطەى   wasté: bə ---i by means of

واتا   watá that is to say, that is

واتـ   waté word; statement. bə ---yek-i tĭr
in other words

واوا   wawá curse

واز   waz subject, topic of conversation. ---
lə...henán to change the subject from...;
to leave, abandon; to give up, renounce,
quit

وينه   wené reflection; picture, portrait; example;
type. ---i tó (people) like you. bə ---
unparalleled, unique. bo --- for example

وينەكر   wenagír photographer

ويسران   werán¹ ruin, ruination. --- b. to be
ruined, destroyed. máḻtan --- be darn
you!

ويسران   werán² (wer-) (foll. by subjunct.) to have

the courage, dare to (do s.th.)

ویرانـــ   weranə́ ruins

ویـــرانــی   weraní destruction, demolition, ruination

وه   wə; normally suffixed: -u (after cons.),
-w (after wovel) and. wənə́be (foll. by
subjunct.) it is not that...

وه عـــد   weʕd promise; appointment. --- d. to
make a promise

وه هـــا   wəhá thus, so, like this (=wa). bə
jorek-i -́- in such a way as this. hər
--- similarly, in the same way. ---...kə
such... as... šīt -́- drust ʔəkat kə
tənanə́t bə xə́xiš nə̀tdiwə he is building
(such) things that you haven't even dreamed
of

وه جـــاخ   wəjáx male offspring, sons

وه ك   wə́k, wə́ku as such as, like. Foll. by subjunct.: as if, as though. hər -́- Foll.
by subjunct.: as if, as though

وه كـــی كه   wəkiké on the other hand

وه كــو   wə́ku like, as. --- wū́tman as we have
said. wə́ku...wá just like; with foll.
subjunct.: just as if. wəku ʔə́mə wáyə
it is just like this one. --- ʔəmbini wám
I am just as you see me. --- ʔə́m ʕaləmè
həmúy ʔasīn-i sárd bĭkute wáys just as
if all these people were hammering on cold
iron

وه ك یـ ك   wəkyə́k similar; without difference

وه لا م   wəlám reply, answer. ---i...d.əwə́ to
answer (a question)

وه لـلا هـــی   wə́llahi by God! indeed!

وه نـه و شـــ   wənəwšə́ a kind of flower

وه قتـــی   wəqtí temporary

وەر	**wər** away (preverbal particle, occurring with verbs to form verbal phrases, which are listed under the verb in question)
وەرام	**wərám = wəlám** answer. --- d.əwə to reply, answer
وەرچەرخاو	**wərčərxáw** change; reversed
وەرگرتن	**wərgi̇́rti̇́n** taking, winning
وەرین	**wərín** (wər-) to come loose; to fall down
وەرزین	**wərzén** sports
وەرزش	**wərzi̇́š** sports; physical education
وەرین	**wəřín** (wəř-) to bark
وەرس بون	**wəřs bún** to get bored
وەستا	**wəstá** master craftsman. ---yanə like a master, masterfully
وەستان	**wəstán** (wəst-) to stand. bə... to stop (doing s.th.). bərambər --- to stand before, encounter, stand up to. řa --- to stop (motion); to stand, stand up. řá wəstə stop! halt! ʔotombiləkə řá wəstawə the car is waiting
راوشاندن	**wəšandín** (wəšen-): řa --- to shake (trans.)
وطنی	**wətení** national
وەخت بە سەر بردن	**wəxi̇́tbəsərbi̇́rdín** bə... killing time, whiling away time by, with...
وەخت	**wəxt, wéxi̇́t** time. ---əkéy at that time. ---́-e, lə ---́-ekda (at the time) when. --- bi̇́rdnəsér to kill time
وەختی	**wəxtí** temporary
وەی	**wəy** (exclam.) woe! --- mín woe is me!
وەزارەت	**wəzarét** ministry (govt.). ---i daxliyé ministry of the interior

176

وەظیفه wəzifé office, job

وەزیر wəzír minister (of state)

وەزن wézĭn harm, damage. --- henán bə... to harm, do harm to

وەزندەری wəzĭndərí harm; damage

ویستەمەنی wistəməní needs, necessities

ویستن wistĭn, wɪstĭn (pres. stem -ʔwé[t], with subj. indicated by pron. affix inserted before stem, as ʔəməwe[t] 'I want'; pass. stem: wistr-) to want; to need, require. ʔəmém ʔəwet I want this. čít ʔəwe? what do you want? ʔəgər bíəwe if he wants it. ʔəywist bĭřwa he wanted to go. bistu-pénji ʔəwe bo nó it is twenty-five to nine. pe --- to be necessary. pey náwe it is not necessary

وو wĭ-: see also wʊ-

ووچان wʊčán rest; a short period of rest. be --- constantly, without pause

وجود wʊjúd existence

ولات wʊlát nation, state, country. ---əyə̀k-gĭřtuəkàn-i ʔəmərá the United States of America

وون بوون wʊn bún[1] to be lost (le: from the sight of). ʔəgər bə tónya bĭřom --- ʔəbĭm if I go alone I'll get lost. lə čaw --- b. to disappear from sight. --- bú lost

وون بون wʊnbún[2] loss; disappearance

وورد wʊrd fine; very small; tiny; minute; sensitive; delicate; child. --- binín, --- b.əwé to examine critically, scrutinize. --- k.əwé to change money (into small change)

وورد ه به رد wʊrdəbérd little stones; small pieces of stone

ورده ورده wʊrdé wʊrdə̀ bit by bit, slowly, gradually

به وردی wʊrdí: bə --- carefully, closely

ورد وخاش کردن wʊrduxas k. to smash, crush, smash to pieces

وره به ردان wʊré: --- bər d. to be demoralized

وورگ wʊrg stomach; belly

وور شه دار wʊršədár rustling

وورت wʊrtə́ word; muttering, mumbling (n.); any sound emitted through the mouth. --- lə dəmma náyetə dəre I won't make a sound

وور یا wʊryá smart, bright, astute; careful, cautious. ---...b. to be careful of

وور بوون wʊřbún dizziness, giddiness, vertigo

وو س wʊs silent

وشه wʊšə́ word

ووشک wʊ́šĭk dry. --- b. to dry up

ووتار wʊtár speech, talk; essay, article (ləsər: on). --- xwendnəwə́ to deliver a speech

ووته wʊtə́ word; saying, utterance; statement. ---i qút witty conversation

ووتن wʊtĭn (le-; pass. stem wʊtr-) to say. ʔəley čĭ bĭin... how about going...? ʔəley, ʔətwút you would say, one might say, as if. be...---,... ... pe --- to call s.o. s.th. ʔəmə čĭ pe ʔələn? what do they call this?

وتنه وه wʊtnəwə́ (le-) to repeat s.th.; to teach, instruct

ووتسو کردن wʊtú k. to iron, press

ووتسو چی wʊtucí launderer

لسه وزه بوون wʊzá: lə ---da b. (foll. by subjunct.) to be able to, bear to (do s.th.)

خ   x

خــاك   xák land, earth

خالــــد   xalíd Khalid (m.p.n.)

خــال   xal uncle (maternal). kuř-i -́-, kǐč-i -́͂ cousin

خالـج ى ريـوار   xalə-i řebwar a Kurdish song (calling to a man on a journey: "O! you traveler!")

خالـوژن   xaložín mother's brother's wife

خـــام   xam canvas; calico

خـــامه   xamé pen; pencil. bə ---i by the pen of, by

خـــاموش   xamóš quiet

خـــان   xan¹ caravansary; inn

خـــان   xan² Khan (title of respect following woman's maiden name or man's first name). məhmú -́--i dǐzlí Mahmoud Khan of Dizli

خانـــقا   xanəqá mosque (usually large, with a large religious school)

خانقـــين   xanəqín Khanaqin (town on Iranian frontier)

خانـــوو   xanú house

خاسـه ته ن   xasətén especially

خــــاو   xaw melting. xəyáli xáwə his dreams are evaporating

خاوين   xawén clean, tidy, trim

خاوه ن   xawén owner, proprietor

خاوه ن ئه خلاق   xawənʔəxláq person of fine character

خاوه ن پاره   xawènparé wealthy, rich

خاوه ن شكــو   xawənškó his majesty. --- qəysér His Majesty the Czar

خاوه‌ن خیزان	xawənxezán head of a family, householder
خاولـــــی	xawlí towel
خـــیل	xél̲ tribe
خـــــیر	xer blessings, well-being. bə -́-́ beyt, bə -́-́ hati welcome. bə --- či goodbye. qĭsəyek-i --- a good word (on behalf of s.o.)
خـــــیرا	xerá fast, quickly
به‌ خـــیرایی	xeraí: bə --- quickly, rapidly
خـــــیزان	xezán family; wife
خه‌بات	xəbát struggle, contention. --- k. to struggle. -́-́-i kĭrduwəw ʔəyká he has struggled and is struggling
خه‌باتكه‌ر	xəbatkér the person who struggles
خه‌فــــت	xəfét sadness; sorrow
خه‌فه‌ت باری	xəfətbarí great sorrow, grief
خه‌لـــیفه	xəlifé Caliph
خه‌لك ، خه‌لـــق	xəlk, xəl̲k, xəlq, xél̲ĭk people; inhabitants. həmí -́-́ all the people. to ---i kwey? where are you from? -́-́ə, -́-́inə (voc.) O people!
خه‌لـــــوز	xəl̲úz charcoal. ---i bérd coal
خــــم	xém grief. -́-́ĭt nébe have no fear!
خمســـه	xəmsé five. həwas-i -́-́ the five senses
خه‌نجه‌ر	xənjér dagger
خه‌ریك	xərík busy at, engaged in, occupied in. ---i...b. to be busy at, busy (doing s.th.). Foll. by subjunct.: to be about to (do s.th.). ...máɳə ---i ʔĭš kĭrdĭnĭn for months they have been hard at work. ---ə nán bĭwxa he's about to eat. --- k. bə to keep s.o. busy at s.th.

خریطه   xərité map

خەرج   xərj expenditure. --- k. to spend

خەرمەن   xərmén joy; myriads

خەسار   xəsar a loss

خەست   xəst concentrated. čayek-i --- a strong tea

خەستەخانه   xəstəxané hospital

خەسوو   xəsú son's wife's mother

خەت   xət writing, script; handwriting; temper (of steel). ---i bïzmarí cuneiform script

خەتەر   xətér grave, serious

خەو   xəw sleep, nap; dream. ---i naxóš night-mare. --- binín to dream, have a dream. bə -́-iš nə̀ydiwə undreamed of (by him). lə širin,---da b. to be sound asleep. ---y hatïn to become sleepy. -́-m yet I'm sleepy. --- lə...kəwtïn to fall asleep. -́-m lə kəwt I fell asleep. -́-y řəwinəwé (řəw-) not to be sleepy any more. -́-m řəwìyəwə I'm not sleepy any more

خەوتنان   xəwtnán evening; night

خەیال   xəyá̱l idea, thought; imagination. -́- xáwə he is dreaming false dreams. --- k. to think, be pensive. ---i xéw k. to daydream

خەیار   xəyár cucumber

خەزور   xəzúr son's wife's father

خلەخل   xïləxḯl the staggering walk of a child; spinning

خنکان   xïnkán to choke (intr.); to drown (intr.)

خنکاندن   xïnkandḯn hanging; execution; strangu-lation

خسر   xïr round

181

خـــراب xïráp bad. štèk-i xrápe that's too bad! xïráp tè geyštuy you misunderstand!

خـــروشان xïrošán (xroše-) to be agitated, riotous, on a rampage

خستن xïstïn (xe-) to put, place; to drop. da --- to close, shut; to lock; to button. der --- to disclose, display, show, demonstrate; to reveal (bo: to s. o.); to express (an opinion). xoy der --- to make itself evident, become clear. le... to throw s.th. pe le...--- to scrape s.th. with the foot. peš --- to promote, foster, further s.th. řa --- to spread out, lay down (carpet). řaxráw carpeted.ře --- to arrange, prepare for. tek --- to intertwine, interweave. -́-e... to place s.th. in...; to have s.o. enter s.th.; to put off, postpone s.th. to; to cause or make s.o. to be or do s.th. ?iš-i ?ímřo mèxere sbéyne do not leave for tomorrow what you can do today (prov.). gul ?exáte pekenín he makes the flowers laugh. -́-e ber čaw to put before the eye, to bring before the public, publish. ---e ser... to put s.th. on, to load on; to join, add, annex s.th. to. barekéy xïste ser keřeké he put the load on the donkey. ---e peš... to place s.th. before..., give priority to s.th. over...

خشت xïšt brick (standard size). ---i surewekráw baked bricks

خشته xïšté level. le --- bïrdïn to ruin. xóyan le --- bïrduwe they have ruined themselves

خـــزان xïzán (xze-): le...--- to draw near to. zór le žnekéy ?exze he draws very close to his wife

خـــزاندن xïzandín (xze-) to slip

خـــزم xïzïm relative, relatives; people, community

خـــزمت xïzmét service. be ---i ... geyštïn to meet, see (honorific)

182

خـزمەتکـار xïzmətkár servant

خـــو xo¹ (interjection) I say! indeed! well,
now! --- ?əgər bétu... but if, but in the
event that...

خـــو xo² self; the very, original. (normally
occurs with pron. suff.) xom myself.
xoy himself. ?arəzu-i xóte as you wish, it's up
to you. ləsər --- slow and sure, un-
hurriedly. ləbər -´-yəwə within oneself,
to oneself. lə -´-yəwə by itself, auto-
matically. ---y lə -´-ya in itself. lə
wəxt-i ---y at that very time, originally.
bə jega-i ---y in its very own place. hatnə
sər --- to regain consciousness

یا خـــود xod: ya -´- or else; or perhaps

خویی xoí personal, individual (adj.); selfishness, egoism; personal motives

خـــول xoḻ earth, dirt, soil. tənəkə-i ---
garbage can

خولە میش xoḻəméš ash, ashes

خولــە میشاو xoḻəmešáw a mixture of ashes and water

خولــە میشی xoḻəmeší gray

خوپە رست xopərḯst selfish

خوپە سەندی xopəsəɲí selfishness

خـــور xor¹ sun

خـــور xor² eater; drinker. kəm ---i daym ---bə
eat little but often (prov.)

خـوراوا xor?awá, xorawá west

خوررایی xořaí free, gratis

خوراکیشان xořakešán dragging oneself (n.)

خـــوش xoš pleasant, nice. bə xwa -´-ə my, how
nice! --- b. bə... to be pleased by.
dïlman ---bu bə hatïnman bo máltan we are
veřy happy to visit you. lə...---b. to have

mercy on, forgive s.o.; to find s.o.
pleasant. xwa le -́--bu God have mercy on
him. pe --- b. to find pleasant, like
s.th. ʔerém pe xóšɘ I like it here.
ʔemɘ zórman pe ---ɘ kɘ... we are very happy
that... --- k. to make it pleasant; to fan.
xwa -́-ït kɘ [fine], thank you (response to
inquiry on one's health). --- wistín to
love. tom -́-- ʔɘwe I love you

خوش به ختی   xošbɘxtí good fortune, luck. mayɘ-i ---
a stroke of good luck

خوشه ویست   xošɘwíst beloved, dear; respected (when
used with names of newspapers, etc.)

خوشهاتن کردن   xošhatïn k. to welcome

خوشحال   xošḫál happy, pleased

خوشی   xoší happiness, pleasure, joy. bɘ ---
happily

خوشیوتالسی   xošiwtalí prosperity and distress

خوخور   xoxór cannibal

خوزگــــه   xozgé I wish, I hope, would that...
Foll. by pres. subjunct. = a possible
wish, foll. by imperf. indic. = a wish
unlikely to be fulfilled. --- lém
bïtïrsïn I hope they're afraid of me.
--- jàrek-i tïriš ʔɘhàtitɘwɘ náwman I
wish you could come and live among us
again

خـــرایی   xraí: -́--tan pe ʔɘkɘm approx.: I'll
take care of you!

خـراپ   xrap bad

خـراپه   xrapé badness, evil

خـــو   xu behavior, manners; habit, custom

خـــوری   xurí wool

تی خوردان   te...xuřán (xuř-) to call to...

خـــول   xυl a turn; a revolution. --- d. to

revolve. --- xwardín to revolve, spin around; to orbit

خوله هاتن   xʋléı: ---y hatín to walk about from one place to another

خـــول   xʋlé² Khula (nickname for Mahmoud, Muhammad)

خولقاند ن   xʋlqandín (xʋlqe-) to be created

خول_يا   xʋlyá worry, disturbing thought

خومــار   xʋmár drunkenness. čáwi bə -́-ə his eyes are unstable (from drinking)

لى خورين   xʋrín (xʋr-): le --- to drive (a vehicle). mĭn trʋmbél le ʔəxʋrĭm I (can) drive a car

خورمـا   xʋrmá date(s) (fruit)

خورمال   xʋrmál Khurmal (a nahya in Sul. Liwa). ---i kon Old Khurmal

خوشك   xʋšk sister. xʋ́škə, xʋ́ške (voc., title of respect for women) sister! Madame! -́-ə nəsrín Sister Nasrin!

خوشكه بچوك   xʋškəbcʋ́k younger sister

خو شكه كه وره   xʋškəgəwré elder sister

خو شكه زا   xʋškəzá sister's son/daughter, nephew, niece

خطـوات   xʋtwát steps; measures

خـــوا   xwa God. --- hafíz goodbye. ---t ləgél goodbye (said to one leaving)

خـوا ه ناس   xwaənás God-fearing; theist

خـــواجا   xwajá title of respect for Jews. --- mʋšé Mr. Moses

خـــوان   xwan dining table

خـــوار   xwar bottom; below, following. bə ---iəwə below it; to the south of it. xwáre down. xwárəwə down; downstairs

خواردەمەنسى   xwardəməní   food

خواردن   xwardín¹   to eat; to pester s.o.; often used idiomatically in the sense of to undergo, suffer, receive (misfortune, etc.). ta ʔə́m həmù tehəldanə̀ším néxwardïbu   so that I wouldn't have suffered all of this beating

خواردن   xwardín²   food; eating (n.). kəbáb čaktrín ---ə lerə.   kebob is the best food here

خواردنەوە   xwardnəwé¹   to drink

خواردنەوە   xwardnəwé²   drinking (n.); (alcoholic) beverages

خواری   xwáre   down

خوارەوە   xwárəwə   down(ward)(s); downstairs

خواروو   xwarú   south

خواست   xwast   request, entreaty

خواستن   xwastín (xwaz-)   to want, desire. xwá néxwastə   God forbid

خواوند   xwawénd   almighty

خواخوا بوون   xwaxwa-i...b.   to wait impatiently for... ---i ʔəwəy bu kat xerá bïrwa   he was impatiently waiting for time to pass

خواز   xwaz   a wish; partisan. ʔašt-i ---án   peace partisans

خوی   xwe   salt

خوین   xwen   blood. --- wʊn b.   one's blood goes unavenged

خوێندەوار   xwendəwár   reader (person); literate; educated person

خوێندەواری   xwendəwarí   literacy; learning, knowledge

خوێندن   xwendín (xwend-)   to read; to study; to sing. dərs ---   to study

خويندنه وه   xwendnəwə́ (xwen-) to read again; to read s.th. back (to s.o.)

خوينه خوى   xwenəxwə́ avenger, revenge seeker; vindictive

خوينگرم   xwengə́rĭm hot-blooded; vehement

ى   y

يا ، يان   ya, yan or. ---...--- either or. -´-bə papòr -´- bə təyarə́ by either ship or plane. wə yá, wə yán or else. After neg.: nor. ---ná, ---nə́? or not. yáxwa (foll. by subjunct.) I hope (formula). -´-xwa řastbe I hope that's right

ياد   yad commemoration, anniversary; reminiscence. ---i sesalə́ the third anniversary. henánə --- to řecall, remember

يان   yan or. See 'ya'

يانه   yanə́ club (social). ---i fərmanbərán the Officials' Club

يانسى   yáni = yəʕní that is to say, that is

يانزه   yanzə́ eleven

ياپراخ   yaprád cabbage leaves stuffed with rice and meat

يار   yar friend

يارى   yarí game; play. --- k. to play (a game); to make a move (in a game)

ياريكر   yarikə́r player

يارمەتى   yarmətí help; assistance. --- d. to help

ياسا   yasá law; statute; system of regulations

ييشان   yešán (yeš-) to ache, hurt s.o. lášĭm ʔəmyeše my side also hurts (me). sə́rĭm ʔəyeša I had a headache

یه عنی	yərní, yaní it means; that is to say, i.e.
یه ك	yək (=yek) one; each other (=yəktír). bə ---əwə both, all of them; together. yékek a person; someone. yəkəmín first. hər---é everyone. ---dú one or two. --- b. to bə one, be (both) the same. sĭnúrišyan ---be... that their boundaries should be the same. bə --- gəyštín to arrive together, meet. --- gĭrtín to come together, get together, unite; to agree. nətəwəyəkgĭrtuwəkán the United Nations. --- xĭstín to unify, unite s.th. čúnə --- to become smaller, shrink. k. bə --- to unite, unify s.th.
یه ك دل	yəkdíl united
یه كیك	yékek a person, one, someone; (foll. by subjunct.) anyone who. ---i ké another one, someone else
یه كیتی	yəketí unity, union; unanimity. -----sovyét the Soviet Union
یكه یكه	yəké: --- --- one by one, individually
یه كم ، یه كه مین	yəkém, yəkəmín first. bo jar-i yəkém, yəkəmin jar for the first time
یه ك گــرتن	yəkgĭrtín unification
یه كگرتنه وه	yəkgĭrtnəwé re-unification
یه ك گرتــوو	yəkgĭrtú united, unified
به یه كجاری	yəkjarí: bə --- completely, totally
یه ك كه وتن	yəkkəwtín agreement, concurrence
یه كســر	yəksér directly, straight
یه كشه مه	yəkšəmmé Sunday
یه كتر	yəktír each other
یه كخستن	yəkxĭstín unification
یــزدان	yəzdán Yazdan, God
یه زیــدی	yəzidí Yezidi

188

يونانستان   yunanĭstán   Greece

يـورانـــيوم   yuranyóm   uranium

ژ   z

زانـــا   zaná[1]   learned; educated; scholar, scientist

زانـــا   zaná[2]   Zana (m.p.n.)

زانـــين   zanín[1] (zan-) to know; to come to know, find out. nàzanĭm čónbu I don't know how it happened that... hər ʔəwəndém zanì before I realized it, suddenly. bə...--- to feel, sense, be aware of; foll. by subjunct.: to consider it...(to do s.th.). bə pewístĭm nəzanì břom. I didn't think it necessary to go. bə báṧĭm nəzanì břom I did not think it well to go. wa --- to believe, suppose, imagine. wá bzanĭm I believe, I suppose. wám zanì I thought, it was my belief...

بوزانـــين   zanín[2]: bo --- announcement, notice

زانستگه   zanĭstgé, zanĭstgá   university

زانستــــى   zanĭstí   teaching, instruction

زانـــراو   zanráw   finding, discovery

زانـــيار   zanyár   erudite; learned person

زانـــياری   zanyarí   knowledge, education. wəzìr-i -́-   the Minister of Education

زاراو   zaráw   dialect

زارولـــ   zaroḻé   child

ژاوا   zawá   husband; father's sister's husband; daughter's husband

زايەلـــ   zayəḻé   echo

زيـــر   zer   gold

زیلـــکاو	zelkáw marsh
زیرینـــوك	zeřinók Zerinok (place name)
زهعیف	zeʕíf thin. lam-i -́- the "clear" l (as opp. to the velar l)
زهبـــر	zəbr power; force
زهحمهت	zəhmét difficulty, trouble; difficult. bə ‾-́--i mézanə don't consider it a bother = please (request)
زهلــم.	zəlím Zalim (a river in Sul. Liwa)
زهمان	zəmán time, era
زهمین	zəmín earth; globe
زهنگ	zéŋ bell
زهنـــگین	zəŋgín rich. ---trín richest
زهراعـــت	zəraʕét agriculture
زهرد	zərd yellow
زهردهوالـــ	zərdəwalé wasp; hornet
زهردهخهنه	zérdəxəné smile; smiling (n.). --- gĭrtín, --- k. to smile
زهردهشتی	zərədəští Zoroastrian; Zoroastrianism
زهرهنگهری	zərəŋərí goldsmithery
زهرف	zérĭf envelope (mail)
زهرقـــی	zərqí green; youthful
زهرر	zəř braying (of donkeys)
زهرره	zəřé a very small particle; atom
زهررین	zəřín wasp
زریه	zəřɪyé, zuřɪyé atomic. qĭnbĭlə-i --- atomic bomb
زهوی	zəwí earth; land; plot of land

190

زویر بوون لــ lə...zəwir b. to be angry with. létan --- ʔəbe he will be angry with you

زه وی وزار zəwiwzár arable land

زه وق zə̀wq taste; sensitivity. bə --́-mə it is to my taste

زه وقــی zəwqí happiness

زه وت کــردن zə̀wt k. to invade; to take away by force, usurp

زین zin saddle

زیندهگانی zindəganí liveliness, animation, state of being alive

زیندو zindú, ziŋú living, alive. --- k.əwə́ to revive. wə́xtə mïrdúyš --́- bïkənəwə they are even on the point of bringing the dead back to life

به زیندویی zinduí state of being alive. bə --- alive, while alive

زینهت zinə́t Zinat (f.p.n.)

زیرهك zirə́k clever; intelligent

زیت zít agile; quick

زیخ zíx small pebble, gravel

زیــز ziz angry, vexed

زگ = ســك zïg = sïg, sïk stomach. ---y čun to have diarrhoea

زکــماك zïkmák congenital

زل zïl great, large

زمــان zïmán tongue; language

زینده به چال zïndə bə čál burying alive

زنجیر zïnjír chain; series; chains, manacles

زرنگانهوه zïrïŋanəwə́ (zrïŋe-) to ring, rattle; to resound

191

زرمــه	zïrmé explosion; blast
زروف	zïrúf circumstances, conditions
زر	zïř tree that gives no fruit
زربـــرا	zïřbrá step-brother
زرخوشـــك	zïř xúšk step-sister
رستـــان	zïstán winter
زيافـــت	zıyafét banquet, dinner
زيان	zıyán damage, disadvantage; harm; loss
زور	zor¹ force. bə --- by force. --- lə...k. (foll. by subjunct.) to force s.o. to (do s.th.)
زور	zor² much; a lot; many; very; too, too much. ---yan kïři they bought a lot. --- mʊhəndís many engineers. --- baše (that's) very good; very well! --- pem xòše it pleases me very much. --- b. to grow larger, increase (intrans.). --- pe čun to take long; neg.: to lose no time, not to delay. zóri pe néču he did not delay; without delay, he... --- k. to make larger, increase, augment s.th.
زوردارى	zordarí oppression
زورى	zorí great amount, abundance. bə --- for the most part
زرى	zře tinkling sound (of coins, glass, etc.)
زو	zú early; soon. --- lə bəyaní hélsta he got up early in the morning. --- pey wʊt he told him right away. bém---wanə in the next few days
زوويـــى	zuí: bə --- speedily, quickly
زبـــان	zʊbán = zïmán tongue; language
زوبانــــى	zʊbaní pertaining to the language; linguistic

زوبان شناس   zuban šunás   one who knows the language

زولــم   zulm injustice

زوربـــه   zurbé most, the greatest part of, majority.
---i... the majority of, most of

ظـــروف   zurúf (pl. of zərf) circumstances; utensils

زیاتـــر   zya, zyad more (n.). lə...zyatïr more ﹀
than. lə də zyatïr more than ten. zyatïr
lə həmí most of all

زیاد   zyad = zya more, additional; a larger
amount. lémbabetèwə agadarí- --- more
attention to this matter. --- k. to in-
crease, augment s.th.

ژ   ž

ژان   žan ache, pain, agony

ژانه سه ر   žanəsér headache

ژاپــــون   žapón Japan

ژیـــر   žer bottom; under. lə ---...da under,
beneath. lə ---...əwə from under

ژیـردەستە   žerdəsté under the control of s.o.; sub-
jugated; subordinate, subject (of a ruler)

ژیـــن   žín living, life

ژیـــر   žir astute, sage; well-behaved (children).
mïnal bə...---k. to make children behave
by... (frightening, etc.)

ژیشك   žišïk hedgehog

ژماردن به   žïmardín (žmer-) to count. --- bə to
consider...as

ژمـــاره   žïmaré number, numeral; number, issue (of
a periodical)

ژن   žïn woman; wife

žĭnbrá

زنبرا	žĭnbrá wife's brother
ژن هينان	žĭnhenán (hen-) to get married (to a woman)
ژیان	žɪyán[1] (žy-, ž-) to live; to live (lə: in a place). bĭží bravo!
ژیان	žɪyán[2] life; living (n.); lifetime
ژور	žur room
ژوری	žúre inside, into
ژوره وه	žúrəwə inside. lə -́-yə it is inside
ژورو	žurú north
ژیان	žyan = žɪyán life, being, existence